T0222149

Data Processing on FPGAs

Synthesis Lectures on Data Management

Editor
M. Tamer Özsu, *University of Waterloo*

Synthesis Lectures on Data Management is edited by Tamer Özsu of the University of Waterloo. The series will publish 50- to 125 page publications on topics pertaining to data management. The scope will largely follow the purview of premier information and computer science conferences, such as ACM SIGMOD, VLDB, ICDE, PODS, ICDT, and ACM KDD. Potential topics include, but not are limited to: query languages, database system architectures, transaction management, data warehousing, XML and databases, data stream systems, wide scale data distribution, multimedia data management, data mining, and related subjects.

Data Processing on FPGAs
Jens Teubner and Louis Woods
2013

Perspectives on Business Intelligence
Raymond T. Ng, Patricia C. Arocena, Denilson Barbosa, Giuseppe Carenini, Luiz Gomes, Jr. Stephan Jou, Rock Anthony Leung, Evangelos Milios, Renée J. Miller, John Mylopoulos, Rachel A. Pottinger, Frank Tompa, and Eric Yu
2013

Semantics Empowered Web 3.0: Managing Enterprise, Social, Sensor, and Cloud-based Data and Services for Advanced Applications
Amit Sheth and Krishnaprasad Thirunarayan
2012

Data Management in the Cloud: Challenges and Opportunities
Divyakant Agrawal, Sudipto Das, and Amr El Abbadi
2012

Query Processing over Uncertain Databases
Lei Chen and Xiang Lian
2012

Foundations of Data Quality Management
Wenfei Fan and Floris Geerts
2012

© Springer Nature Switzerland AG 2022
Reprint of original edition © Morgan & Claypool 2013

All rights reserved. No part of this publication may be reproduced, stored in a retrieval system, or transmitted in any form or by any means—electronic, mechanical, photocopy, recording, or any other except for brief quotations in printed reviews, without the prior permission of the publisher.

Data Processing on FPGAs

Jens Teubner and Louis Woods

ISBN: 978-3-031-00721-7   paperback
ISBN: 978-3-031-01849-7   ebook

DOI 10.1007/978-3-031-01849-7

A Publication in the Springer series
SYNTHESIS LECTURES ON DATA MANAGEMENT

Lecture #35
Series Editor: M. Tamer Özsu, *University of Waterloo*
Series ISSN
Synthesis Lectures on Data Management
Print 2153-5418   Electronic 2153-5426

Data Processing on FPGAs

Jens Teubner
Databases and Information Systems Group, Dept. of Computer Science, TU Dortmund

Louis Woods
Systems Group, Dept. of Computer Science, ETH Zürich

SYNTHESIS LECTURES ON DATA MANAGEMENT #35

ABSTRACT

Roughly a decade ago, power consumption and heat dissipation concerns forced the semiconductor industry to radically change its course, shifting from sequential to parallel computing. Unfortunately, improving performance of applications has now become much more difficult than in the good old days of frequency scaling. This is also affecting databases and data processing applications in general, and has led to the popularity of so-called *data appliances*—specialized data processing engines, where software and hardware are sold together in a closed box. Field-programmable gate arrays (FPGAs) increasingly play an important role in such systems. FPGAs are attractive because the performance gains of specialized hardware can be significant, while power consumption is much less than that of commodity processors. On the other hand, FPGAs are way more flexible than hard-wired circuits (ASICs) and can be integrated into complex systems in many different ways, e.g., directly in the network for a high-frequency trading application. This book gives an introduction to FPGA technology targeted at a database audience. In the first few chapters, we explain in detail the inner workings of FPGAs. Then we discuss techniques and design patterns that help mapping algorithms to FPGA hardware so that the inherent parallelism of these devices can be leveraged in an optimal way. Finally, the book will illustrate a number of concrete examples that exploit different advantages of FPGAs for data processing.

KEYWORDS

FPGA, modern hardware, database, data processing, stream processing, parallel algorithms, pipeline parallelism, programming models

Contents

Preface

System architectures, hardware design, and programmable logic (specifically, *field-programmable gate arrays* or *FPGAs*) are topics generally governed by electrical engineers. "Hardware people" are in charge of embracing technological advantages (and turning them into improved performance), preferably without breaking any of the established hardware/software interfaces, such as instruction sets or execution models.

Conversely, computer scientists and software engineers are responsible for understanding users' problems and satisfying their application and functionality demands. While doing so, they hardly care how hardware functions underneath—much as their hardware counterparts are largely unaware of how their systems are being used for concrete problems.

As time progresses, this traditional separation between hard- and software leaves more and more potential of modern technology unused. But giving up the separation and building *hardware/software co-designed systems* requires that both parties involved understand each other's terminology, problems/limitations, requirements, and expectations.

With this book we want to help work toward this idea of co-designed architectures. Most importantly, we want to give the software side of the story—the database community in particular—a basic understanding of the involved hardware technology. We want to explain what FPGAs are, how they can be programmed and used, and which role they could play in a database context.

This book is intended for students and researchers in the database field, including those that have not had much contact with hardware technology in the past, but would love to get introduced to the field. At ETH Zürich/TU Dortmund, we have been teaching for several years a course titled "Data Processing on Modern Hardware." The material in this book is one part of that Master-level course (which further discusses also "modern hardware" other than FPGAs).

We start the book by highlighting the urgent need from the database perspective to invest more effort into hardware/software co-design issues (Chapter 1). Chapters 2 and 3 then introduce the world of electronic circuit design, starting with a high-level view, then looking at FPGAs specifically. Chapter 3 also explains how FPGAs work internally and why they are particularly attractive at the present time.

In the remaining chapters, we then show how the potential of FPGAs can be turned into actual systems. First, we give general guidelines how algorithms and systems can be designed to leverage the potential of FPGAs (Chapter 4). Chapter 5 illustrates a number of examples that successfully used FPGAs to improve database performance. But FPGAs may also be used to enable new database functionality, which we discuss in Chapter 7 by example of a database crypto co-processor. We conclude in Chapter 8 with a wary look into the future of FPGAs in a database context.

A short appendix points to different flavors of FPGA system integration, realized through different plug-ins for commodity systems.

Jens Teubner and Louis Woods
June 2013

CHAPTER 1

Introduction

For decades, performance of sequential computation continuously improved due to the stunning evolution of microprocessors, leaving little room for alternatives. However, in the mid-2000s, power consumption and heat dissipation concerns forced the semiconductor industry to radically change its course, shifting from sequential to parallel computing. Ever since, software developers have been struggling to achieve performance gains comparable to those of the past. Specialized hardware can increase performance significantly at a reduced energy footprint but lacks the necessary flexibility. FPGAs (reprogrammable hardware) are an interesting alternative, which have similar characteristics to specialized hardware, but can be *(re)programmed* after manufacturing. In this chapter, we give an overview of the problems that commodity hardware faces, discuss how FPGAs differ from such hardware in many respects, and explain why FPGAs are important for data processing.

1.1 MOORE'S LAW AND TRANSISTOR-SPEED SCALING

Ever since Intel co-founder Gordon E. Moore stated his famous observation that the number of transistors on integrated circuits (IC) doubles roughly every two years, this trend (*Moore's law*) has continued unhalted until the present day. The driving force behind Moore's law is the continuous miniaturization of the *metal oxide semiconductor* (MOS) transistor, the basic building block of electronic circuits. Transistor dimensions have been shrunk by about 30 % every two years, resulting in an area reduction of 50 %, and hence the doubling of transistors that Moore observed.

Transistor scaling has not only led to more transistors but also to *faster* transistors (shorter delay times and accordingly higher frequencies) that consume *less energy*. The bottom line is that, in the past, every generation of transistors has enabled circuits with twice as many transistors, an increased speed of about 40 %, consuming the same amount of energy as the previous generation, despite 50 % more transistors. The theory behind this technology scaling was formulated by Dennard et al. [1974] and is known as *Dennard's scaling*. There was a time when Dennard's scaling accurately reflected what was happening in the semiconductor industry. Unfortunately, those times have passed for reasons that we will discuss next.

1.2 MEMORY WALL AND VON NEUMANN BOTTLENECK

Just like CPUs, off-chip dynamic memory (DRAM) has also been riding Moore's law but due to economic reasons with a different outcome than CPUs. Whereas memory density has been doubling every two years, access speed has improved at a much slower pace, i.e., today, it takes several hundred CPU cycles to access off-chip memory. DRAM is being optimized for large capacity at minimum cost, relying on data locality and caches in the CPU for performance. Thus, a significant gap between processor speed and memory speed has been created over the years, a phenomenon known as the *memory wall*.

Furthermore, the majority of computers today are built according to the *Von Neumann model*, where data and software programs are stored in the same external memory. Thus, the bus between main memory and the CPU is shared between program instructions and workload data, leading to the so-called *Von Neumann bottleneck*.

To mitigate the negative effects of both the *memory wall* and the *Von Neumann bottleneck*, CPUs use many of the available transistors to implement all sorts of acceleration techniques to nonetheless improve performance, e.g., out-of-order execution, branch prediction, pipelining, and last but not least cache hierarchies. In fact, nowadays a substantial amount of transistors and die area (up to 50 %) are used for caches in processors.

1.3 POWER WALL

In the past, *frequency scaling*, as a result of transistor shrinking, was the dominant force that increased performance of commodity processors. However, this trend more or less came to an end about a decade ago. As already mentioned in the previous section, the advantages of higher clock speeds are in part negated by the *memory wall* and *Von Neumann bottleneck*, but more importantly, *power consumption* and *heat dissipation* concerns forced the semiconductor industry to stop pushing clock frequencies much further.

Higher power consumption produces more heat, and heat is the enemy of electronics. Too high temperatures may cause an electronic circuit to malfunction or even damage it permanently. A more subtle consequence of increased temperature is that transistor speed decreases, while current leakage increases, producing even more heat. Therefore, silicon chips have a fixed power budget, which microprocessors started to exeed in the mid-2000s, when frequency scaling hit the so-called *power wall*.

A simplified equation that characterizes CPU power consumption (P_{CPU}) is given below. We deliberately ignore additional terms such as *short circuit* and *glitch* power dissipation, and focus on the most important components: *dynamic power* and *static power*.

$$P_{CPU} = \underbrace{\alpha \times C \times V_{dd}^2 \times f_{clk}}_{\text{dynamic power}} + \underbrace{V_{dd} \times I_{leak}}_{\text{static power}}$$

Dynamic power is the power consumed when transistors are switching, i.e., when transistors are changing their state. The parameter α characterizes the switching activity, C stands for capacitance, V_{dd} for voltage, and f_{clk} corresponds to the clock frequency. *Static power*, on the other hand, is the power consumed even when transistors are inactive, because transistors always leak a certain amount of current (I_{leak}).

As transistors became smaller (< 130 nanometers), reality increasingly started to deviate from Dennard's theory, i.e., the reduced voltage of smaller transistor was no longer sufficient to compensate fully for the increased clock speed and the larger number of transistors. For a number of reasons, voltage scaling could no longer keep up with frequency scaling, leading to excessive power consumption.

Unfortunately, limiting frequency scaling solved the power consumption issue only temporarily. As transistor geometries shrink, a higher percentage of current is leaked through the transistor. As a result, *static power* consumption, which is independent of the clock frequency, is increased. Thus, to avoid hitting the *power wall* again, in the future, an increasing amount of transistors will need to be powered off, i.e., it will only be possible to use a fraction of all available transistors at the same time.

1.4 MULTICORE CPUS AND GPUS

As Moore's law prevailed but frequency scaling reached physical limits, there was a major shift in the microprocessor industry toward parallel computing: instead of aiming for ever-increasing clock frequencies of a single core, multiple identical cores are now placed on the same die. Unfortunately, there are a number of issues with multicore scaling. First of all, performance is now directly dependant on the degree of parallelism that can be exploited for a given task. *Amdahl's law* states that if a fraction f of computation is enhanced by a speedup of S, then the overall speedup is:

$$speedup = \frac{1}{(1 - f) + \frac{f}{S}} \; .$$

In the case of multicores, we can interpret f as the fraction of *parallelizable* computation (assuming perfect parallelization), and S as the number of cores. Thus, as the number of cores increases, so does the pressure to be able to exploit maximum parallelism from a task. However, as Hill and Marty [2008] observed, a parallel architecture that relies on large amounts of homogeneous, lean cores is far from optimal to extract the necessary parallelism from a task. Hill and Marty [2008] suggest that an *asymmetric* architecture would be better suited, while they see the highest potential in *dynamic techniques* that allow cores to work together on sequential execution.

Graphic processors (GPUs), in a sense, are an extreme version of multicore processors. In a GPU there are hundreds of very lean cores that execute code in lockstep. GPUs have the same problems with Almdahl's law as multicore CPUs. In fact, the more primitive GPU cores and the way threads are scheduled on them, reduces flexibility, making it even more difficult to extract suitable parallelism from arbitrary applications that would allow an effective mapping to the GPU architecture.

1.5   SPECIALIZED HARDWARE

Dark silicon [Esmaeilzadeh et al., 2011] refers to the underutilization of transistors due to power consumption constraints and/or inefficient parallel hardware architectures that conflict with Amdahl's law. A promising way to overcome these limitations is a move toward heterogeneous architectures, i.e., where not all cores are equal and tasks are off-loaded to specialized hardware to both improve performance and save energy. This conclusion is similar to the "one size does not fit all" concept [Stonebraker et al., 2007] from database research although applied to hardware architectures.

Instead of mapping a given task to a fixed general-purpose hardware architecture, specialized hardware is mapped to the task at hand. Different problems require different forms of parallelism, e.g., data parallelism versus pipeline parallelism, coarse-grained parallelism vs. fine-grained parallelism. Custom hardware allows employing the most effective form of parallelization that best suits a given task.

Specialized hardware is neither bound to the *Von Neumann bottleneck* nor does it necessarily suffer from the *memory wall*. For instance, custom hardware that needs to monitor network data, e.g., for network intrusion detection or high-frequency trading, can be coupled directly with a hardware Ethernet controller. Thus, the slow detour via system bus and main memory is avoided. Consequently, the need for large caches, branch prediction, etc., dissolves, which saves chip space and reduces power consumption.

Power consumption of specialized hardware solutions is usually orders of magnitude below that of general-purpose hardware such as CPUs and GPUs. Knowing exactly what kind of a problem the hardware is supposed to solve, allows using transistors much more effectively. Also, due to specialized hardware parallelism and avoidance of the *Von Neumann bottleneck*, lower clock frequencies are typically sufficient to efficiently solve a given task, which further reduces power consumption. For instance, a circuit that handles 10G Ethernet traffic processes 64-bit words at a clock speed of only 156.25 MHz.

Nevertheless, specialized hardware also has a number of drawbacks, and in the past systems that were built from custom hardware (e.g. database machines in the 1980s) typically lost the race against systems based on general-purpose hardware. First of all, building custom hardware is a difficult and time-consuming process. Second, potential bugs usually cannot be solved after manufacturing, making testing even more time-consuming, and also increasing the risk associated with producing specialized hardware. Third, unless the custom hardware is mass-produced, it is significantly more expensive than general-purpose hardware. In the past, frequency scaling improved sequential computation performance to such an extent that in many domains custom hardware solutions were simply uneconomical.

1.6 FIELD-PROGRAMMABLE GATE ARRAYS (FPGAS)

Between the two extremes—general-purpose processors and specialized hardware—*reprogrammable hardware* is another class of silicon devices, which in a sense combines the best of both worlds. *Field-programmable gate arrays* (FPGAs) are the most advanced brood of this class. FPGAs consist of a plethora of uncommitted hardware resources, which can be *programmed* after manufacturing, i.e., in the *field*.

A circuit implemented on an FPGA can be thought of as a *hardware simulation* of a corresponding hard-wired circuit. As such FPGA-based circuits exhibit many of the favorable characteristics of specialized hardware: *(i)* application-tailored parallelism, *(ii)* low power-consumption, *(iii)* and integration advantages (e.g., to avoid the *Von Neumann bottleneck*). But the fundamental difference compared to specialized hardware is that circuits implemented on an FPGA can be changed anytime, by a mere update of configuration memory. Of course, there is no free lunch. Hard-wired circuits consume even less energy, require even fewer transistors to implement a given task, and can be clocked faster than FPGAs. But oftentimes these are acceptable (or even negligible) concessions, given the various benefits of *reprogrammability*.

First, reprogrammability allows multiple specialized circuits to execute on the same silicon device in a time-multiplexed manner, i.e., circuits can be "loaded" when they are needed. Second, FPGAs drastically reduce time to market and provide the ability to upgrade already deployed circuits. Third, migration to the next-generation manufacturing process (to benefit from smaller transistors) is seamless, i.e., by buying a next-generation FPGA and migrating the hardware description code, similar to the way software is migrated from one CPU generation to the next.

1.7 FPGAS FOR DATA PROCESSING

Originally, FPGAs were primarily used as *glue logic* on *printed circuit boards* (PCBs), and later on also for rapid prototyping. However, more than two decades of FPGA technology evolution have allowed FPGAs to emerge in a variety of fields, as a class of customizable hardware accelerators that address the increasing demands for performance, with a low energy footprint, at affordable cost. In recent years, increased attention from both academia and industry has been drawn to using FPGAs for *data processing* tasks, which is the domain that this book focuses on.

1.7.1 STREAM PROCESSING

FPGAs have several desirable properties for stream processing applications. High-frequency trading is a good example, where high-rate data streams need to be processed in real time, and microsecond latencies determine success or failure. The I/O capabilities of FPGAs, allow for flexible integration, e.g., in the case of high-frequency trading, the FPGAs are inserted directly into the network, enabling most efficient processing of network traffic. Furthermore, the reprogrammability of FPGAs makes it possible to quickly adapt to market changes.

Another example illustrating the advantages of FPGAs are *network intrusion detection systems* (NIDSs) that scan incoming network packets, attempting to detect malicious patterns. Typically there are several hundred patterns formulated as regular expressions, which all need to be evaluated in real time. The regular expressions can easily be implemented in hardware as *finite state machines* (FSMs), which, on an FPGA, can then all be executed in parallel. Thus, besides the integration and reprogramming capabilities, here the inherent parallelism of FPGAs is exploited to achieve unprecedented performance.

1.7.2 BIG DATA

Data management, in the advent of *big data*, becomes an increasingly difficult task using traditional database techniques. For instance, ad-hoc data analytics queries often cannot rely on indexes, and need to fall back to scanning vast amounts of data. This has led to so-called *data warehouse appliances* that combine hardware and software in a single, closed box, allowing appliance vendors to fine-tune software/hardware co-design. IBM/Netezza's appliance [Francisco, 2011], for example, combines multiple FPGAs and CPUs in a large blade server. To increase I/O bandwidth stored data are highly compressed. During query execution, the FPGAs efficiently decompress and filter data, while the CPUs take care of more complex higher-level operations.

1.7.3 CLOUD COMPUTING

Whereas today FPGAs are still considered exotic for many data processing tasks, *cloud computing* could catapult FPGAs to a mainstream data processing technology. In cloud computing, compute resources are provided as a service to customers, i.e., customers can outsource tasks to the cloud and only pay for the resources they actually need for a particular job. A major cost factor for cloud providers is the *power consumption* of their data centers. Thus, any technology that can deliver the same performance and flexibility with a lower energy footprint is very attractive for the cloud. In addition, big cloud providers such as Google, Amazon, and Microsoft definitively have the economic means to provide a bundle of FPGAs as a service with a high-level programming interface, making FPGA technology much more accessible to customers than it is today. The implications of bringing FPGA acceleration into cloud infrastructures has been discussed, e.g., by Madhavapeddy and Singh [2011].

1.7.4 SECURITY

So far, we stressed *performance* and *energy consumption* as key advantages of FPGAs. However, *security* is a third dimension, where FPGAs can provide significant benefits. FPGA configuration data can be encrypted and authenticated, making it very difficult to tamper with the FPGA configuration itself. These built-in authentication and encryption mechanisms can be used to create a *root of trust*, on top of which secure reprogrammable hardware can be built. In the *Von Neumann model* of a conventional processor, data and program are stored in the same memory, making buffer overflow attacks[1] or rootkits[2] possible. In hardware, on the other hand, data and program can be easily separated, e.g., the program can be implemented in logic (protected by the root of trust), while data are stored in memory. Based on these ideas Arasu et al. [2013] built the *Cipherbase* system, which extends Microsoft's SQL Server with FPGA-based secure hardware to achieve high data confidentiality and high performance.

[1]In a buffer overflow attack, a data buffer's boundary is intentionally overrun such that data are written into adjacent memory. For instance, if the attacker can guess where the program code is stored, this method can be used to inject malicious code.
[2]A rootkit is software that typically intercepts common API calls, and is designed to provide administrator privileges to a user without being detected. A buffer overflow could be exploited to load a rootkit.

CHAPTER 2

A Primer in Hardware Design

Before we delve into core FPGA technology in Chapter 3, we need to familiarize ourselves with a few basic concepts of hardware design. As we will see, the process of designing a hard-wired circuit—a so-called *application specific integrated circuit* (ASIC)—is not that different from implementing the same circuit on an FPGA. In this chapter, we will cover the key components that make up an integrated circuit, how these circuits are typically designed, and the various tools required to convert an abstract circuit specification into a physical implementation, ready for manufacturing.

2.1 BASIC HARDWARE COMPONENTS

The majority of electronic circuits, be it a simple counter or a full-fledged microprocessor, are made up of the following three fundamental ingredients: *(i)* combinational *logic elements*, *(ii) memory elements*, *(iii)* and *wiring* to interconnect logic and memory elements. With the help of a few simple examples, in the following, we will show how these three ingredients are typically combined to construct circuits that implement a given function.

2.1.1 COMBINATIONAL LOGIC

At the heart of any circuit there are basic *logic gates*, which can be combined by wiring their input and output *ports* together to form more complex *combinational logic elements*. For instance, on the left-hand side of Figure 2.1, a circuit known as *half adder* is constructed from an XOR gate and an AND gate. This circuit computes the addition of two one-bit numbers A and B, and reports the result on the output port S. If A and B are both set to one this produces an overflow, which is captured by the AND gate and reported as *carry bit* on output port C. Together with an additional OR gate, two half adders can be combined to build a so-called *full adder*. A full adder has a third input port (*carry-in*) and accounts for the carry bit from another full adder, i.e., it adds up three one-bit numbers. This way, a cascade of full adders can be further combined to construct adders with a wider word width, e.g., 32-bit adders.

Another example of a very fundamental combinational circuit in hardware design is a *multiplexer*, illustrated on the right-hand side of Figure 2.1. This 2-to-1 multiplexer has three input ports: two input signals (in_0, in_1) and a select line (sel) that determines which of the two input signals is routed to the output port of the multiplexer. Again, wider multiplexers can be constructed from these basic 2-to-1 multiplexers. Multiplexers enable the evaluation of conditional

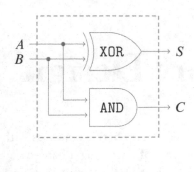
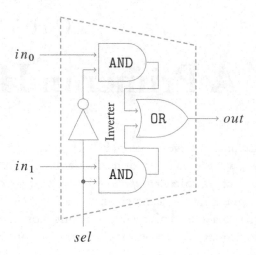

Figure 2.1: Combining basic logic gates to construct more complex circuits: a half adder (left) and a two-input multiplexer (right).

expressions, i.e., *if-then-else* expressions of the form $out = (sel) ? in_1 : in_0$, where sel determines whether in_1 or in_0 is selected for the output.

Combinational logic is purely driven by the input data, i.e., in the examples in Figure 2.1, no clock is involved and no explicit synchronization is necessary. Notice that each logic gate has a fixed *propagation delay*, i.e., the time it takes before the effect of driving input signals is observable at the output of a gate. Propagation delays result from physical effects, such as signal propagation times along a signal wire or switching speeds of transistors. Combining multiple gates increases the overall propagation delay, i.e., the propagation delay of a complex combinational circuit comprises the sum of propagation delays of its gates along the longest path within the circuit, known as the *critical path*. The critical path determines the maximum clock speed of sequential circuits, which we will discuss next.

2.1.2 SEQUENTIAL LOGIC

In contrast to combinational logic, *sequential logic* has state (memory). In fact, sequential logic *is* combinational logic plus memory. While the output of combinational logic depends solely on its present input, the output of sequential logic is a function of both its present and its past input, as illustrated in Figure 2.2 (left). Whereas the *logic gate* is the fundamental building block of combinational logic, *state elements* (e.g., flip-flops, latches, etc.) are the basic building blocks of a sequential circuit.

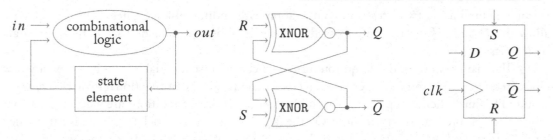

Figure 2.2: A sequential circuit with a feedback loop (left), the internals of an S-R (NOR) latch (center), and symbol of a D flip-flop (right).

2.1.3 ASYNCHRONOUS SEQUENTIAL LOGIC

One of the most basic one-bit state elements is a so-called SR (set/reset) latch. Internally, it can be constructed using two cross-coupled NOR gates, as depicted in Figure 2.2 (center). If S and R are both *logic low* (i.e., $S = 0$, $R = 0$), the feedback loops ensure that Q and $\overline{Q}$ (the complement of Q) remain in a constant state. $S = 1$ and $R = 0$ forces $Q = 1$ and $\overline{Q} = 0$, whereas $S = 0$ and $R = 1$ does the opposite. S and R are not allowed to be *logic high* (i.e., $S = 1$, $R = 1$) at the same time since this would cause $Q = \overline{Q} = 0$.

Notice that the SR latch is *level-sensitive*, meaning that its state changes when the input signals change their voltage *levels* (e.g., where five volt corresponds to one state and zero volt to the other). Thus, even though a circuit with latches can maintain state, it is still entirely driven by its inputs, and no form of *synchronization* exists. Therefore, this type of circuitry is called *asynchronous sequential logic*. The speed of asynchronous sequential logic is essentially only limited by the propagation delays of the logic gates used. However, asynchronous logic is very difficult to get right, with, e.g., race conditions to deal with, which is why nearly all sequential circuits today are *synchronous*.

2.1.4 SYNCHRONOUS SEQUENTIAL LOGIC

In a *synchronous* sequential circuit all memory elements are *synchronized* by means of a *clock* signal, which is generated by an electronic oscillator, and distributed to all memory elements. The clock signal (clk) periodically alternates between two states, i.e., logic low and logic high, and memory elements are synchronized to one of the *clock edges*, i.e. the *rising edge* (change from 0 to 1) or the *falling edge* (change from 1 to 0).

A more sophisticated memory element than the SR latch is required to be able to synchronize to the edge of a clock, e.g., a so-called *D flip-flop*. The symbol that represents a D flip-flop is illustrated on the right-hand side of Figure 2.2. The D flip-flop only stores the input value from the D port at the specified clock edge (rising or falling). After that the outputs (Q and $\overline{Q}$) remain unchanged for an entire clock period (cycle). Internally, the *edge-sensitivity* of D flip-flops is implemented using two latches in combination with additional logic gates. Most D flip-flops allow the D and clk port to be bypassed, forcing the flip-flop to *set* or *reset* state, via separate S/R ports.

The main reason for the ubiquitous use of synchronous sequential logic is its simplicity. The clock frequency determines the length of a clock period and all combinational logic elements are required to finish their computation within that period. If these conditions are met the behaviour of the circuit is predictable and reliable. On the flip-side, maximum clock frequency is determined by the *critical path* in a circuit, i.e., by the longest combinational path between any two flip-flops. As a consequence, the potential performance of other faster combinational elements cannot be maxed out.

2.2   HARDWARE PROGRAMMING

In the early days of electronic circuit design, *schematics* were the only formal way to represent a circuit. Thus, circuits used to be drawn (e.g., as the circuits depicted in Figure 2.1) by hand or using a *computer-aided design* (CAD) tool. Today, the most common way to design a circuit is using an appropriate hardware description language (HDL), which is better suited to capture the complexity of large circuits, and significantly increases productivity.

2.2.1   HARDWARE DESCRIPTION LANGUAGES (HDLS)

The two most popular hardware description languages are Verilog and VHDL (both are also used to program FPGAs). A *hardware description language* (HDL), at first glance, resembles an ordinary programming language such as C. Nevertheless, there are fundamental differences between a language designed for generating assembly code to be executed on a microprocessor, and one that is designed to produce hardware circuits. HDLs are structured programming languages that *(i)* capture circuit hierarchy and connectivity, *(ii)* naturally allow expressing the inherent parallelism of separate circuit components, and *(iii)* provide a built-in mechanism for simulating circuit behavior in software.

Different Levels of Abstraction: Structural versus Behavioral Modeling
The fundamental abstraction in any HDL is a *module* (referred to as *entity* in VHDL). A module encapsulates a (sub)circuit and defines an interface to the outside world in terms of *input/output ports*. Much like classes in an object-oriented language, modules are defined once and can then be instantiated multiple times. Several instantiations of modules execute in parallel and can be connected via wires between their input and output ports.

A Verilog implementation of a 2-to-1 multiplexer (cf. Figure 2.1) is given in Listing 2.1. The module `multiplexer` defines an interface with three single-wire input ports (`in0`, `in1`, `sel`) and one output port (`out`). Inside the multiplexer module four gates are instantiated (1 × inverter, 2 × AND gates, and 1 × OR gate), and connected using the wires `nsel`, `out0` and `out1`. Notice how also the input/output ports of the multiplexer are connected with the instantiated gates.

Listing 2.1: Structural Verilog (MUX).

```
1  module multiplexer (
2    input  in0 , in1 , sel ,
3    output out
4  );
5  wire nsel ;
6  wire out0 ;
7  wire out1 ;
8
9  inverter inv0 ( sel , nsel );
10 andgate  and0 ( in0 , nsel , out0 );
11 andgate  and1 ( in1 , sel , out1 );
12 orgate   or0 ( out0 , out1 , out );
13
14 endmodule
```

Listing 2.2: Behavioral Verilog (MUX).

```
1  module multiplexer (
2    input  in0 , in1 , sel ,
3    output out
4  );
5
6  assign out = sel ? in1 : in0 ;
7
8  endmodule
```

The multiplexer displayed in Listing 2.1 is a *structural* implementation of a 2-to-1 multiplexer. That is, the multiplexer was built *bottom-up* by combining multiple instantiations of simpler modules into a single, more complex module. However, often it is beneficial to model a complex system prior to detailed architecture development. Therefore, common HDLs also support a *top-down* method for designing a circuit, known as *behavioral* modeling. Listing 2.2 shows the same 2-to-1 multiplexer implemented using behavioral Verilog. Whereas structural modeling is an *imperative* technique, exactly defining how a circuit is constructed, behavioral modeling is a *declarative* technique, specifying the behavior rather than the architecture of a circuit.

Simulation

Since producing a hardware circuit is a costly and lengthy process, *simulation* is a crucial tool for designing hardware circuits economically. Simulation is so fundamental that supporting mechanisms are directly integrated into the HDL.

There are various levels of granularity at which a circuit can be simulated. The first step in the design process of a circuit is usually to verify the *behavioral* correctness of a circuit. For that matter, a behavioral model of the circuit is implemented and an appropriate testbench is created within the HDL. A software simulator can then evaluate the circuit against the test cases specified in the testbench.

Later in the design process, *behavioral* components are gradually replaced by *structural* ones, and other aspects than logical correctness, e.g., adherence to timing constraints, become important. HDLs also support this form of simulation, e.g., modules can be annotated with estimated timing information such as propagation delay, etc., and a simulator can check whether a circuit can sustain a given clock rate.

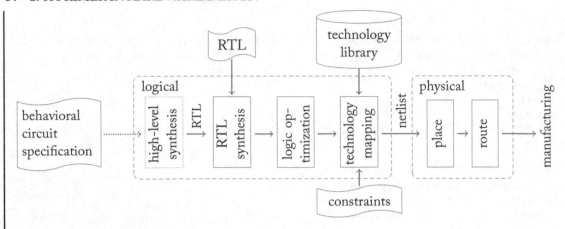

Figure 2.3: Design flow: formal circuit specification → physical circuit.

2.3   CIRCUIT GENERATION

In this section we briefly discuss the design flow for producing a physical circuit from a formal specification, written in some HDL or higher-level language. The main steps are illustrated in Figure 2.3. Most of these steps are also relevant for FPGA programming, which we will discuss in the next chapter.

2.3.1   LOGICAL DESIGN FLOW (SYNTHESIS)

The highest level of abstraction in the circuit design flow are purely *behavioral* specifications of circuits. These specifications are typically not written using a hardware description language. Instead, domain specific languages, as well as standard languages such as C/C++ and SystemC[1] are commonly used. The output of a high-level synthesizer is typically a so-called *register-transfer level* (RTL) description (see below) in HDL code. Notice that high-level synthesis is an active field of research, and especially general-purpose high-level synthesis often produces inferior results, compared to hand-crafted HDL code, which is why RTL descriptions (using, for example, Verilog or VHDL) are still the most common entry point to circuit design.

At the *register-transfer level* (RTL), a circuit is modeled as a network of storage elements (flip-flops, RAMs, etc.) with combinational logic elements in between. At this level, combinational elements may still be specified in a behavioral manner, e.g., an arithmetic adder component may be used, without specifying a concrete implementation of an adder. The RTL abstraction has two immediate advantages: *(i)* increased productivity, as certain functionality can be generated, in contrast to being assembled manually from logic gates, and *(ii)* portability, as the RTL representation is technology independent, e.g., the same RTL specification can be used to generate

---

[1]SystemC is an extension of C++ targeted toward software/hardware co-design.

an ASIC or program an FPGA. To reach an RTL model of a circuit, manual design and tuning may be necessary. However, once an RTL model of a circuit exists, all further processing steps (including RTL synthesis) toward the physical circuit are fully automated.

An RTL synthesizer translates the RTL circuit description into an internal representation of *unoptimized* Boolean logic equations. The next step is a technology-independent optimization of these equations, i.e., redundant logic is automatically removed.

The final step of the synthesis process is to implement the abstract internal representation of the design by mapping it to the *cells* of a *technology library* (also known as *cell library*, provided by the device manufacturer. The cells of a technology library range from basic logic gates (standard cells) to large and complex megacells with ready-to-use layout (e.g., a DMA controller). The library consists of cell descriptions that contain information about functionality, area, timing, and power for each cell. As illustrated in Figure 2.3, the *technology mapping* process also takes *design constraints* into account. These constraints, e.g. regarding area consumption, timing, and power consumption, guide the mapping process, and determine which cells are selected when multiple options exist.

2.3.2 PHYSICAL DESIGN FLOW

The end result of the synthesis process is a so-called *netlist*. Netlists consist of two fundamental components: *instances* and *nets*. Each time a *cell* of some target *technology library* is used, this is called an *instance*. *Nets*, on the other hand, refer to the "wires" that connect instances.

Based on the netlist, the physical design process begins. In the first phase the gates of the netlist are placed on the available two-dimensional space. Initially, structures that should be placed close together are identified—a process known as *floorplanning*. Then, based on the *floorplan*, the *placer tool* assigns a physical location to each gate of the netlist. After initial placement, the *clock tree* is inserted and placement decisions are re-evaluated. Multiple iterations are typically necessary to find a satisfying placement for all gates.

From the *placed-gates* netlist and the geometric information about the cells provided by the technology library, the *router tool* derives the physical paths of the nets that connect gates, as well as the power supply lines. Again, multiple iterations are typically necessary, and gates might be relocated in the routing phase. The fully routed physical netlist is the final result of the entire design flow. It consists of the gates of a circuit, their exact placement, and "drawn" interconnecting wires. In essence, the circuit design is now ready for fabrication. What follows is typically a number of physical design verification steps carried out in software before a first prototype of the circuit is produced by an IC vendor.

C H A P T E R 3

FPGAs

In this chapter, we give an overview of the technology behind *field-programmable gate arrays* (FP-GAs). We begin with a brief history of FPGAs before we explain the key concepts that make (re)programmable hardware possible. We do so in a bottom-up approach, that is, we first discuss the very basic building blocks of FPGAs, and then gradually zoom out and show how the various components are combined and interconnected. We then focus on programming FPGAs and illustrate a typical FPGA design flow, also covering advanced topics such as *dynamic partial reconfiguration*. Finally, to complete the picture of modern FPGAs, we highlight bleeding-edge technology advances and future FPGA trends.

3.1   A BRIEF HISTORY OF FPGAS

Field-programmable gate arrays (FPGAs) arose from *programmable logic devices* (PLDs), which first appeared in the early 1970s. PLDs could be *programmed* after manufacturing in the *field*. However, programmability in these devices was limited, i.e., programmable logic was hard-wired between logic gates.

In 1985, the first commercially available FPGA (the Xilinx XC2064) was invented. This device hosted *arrays* of *configurable logic bocks* (CLBs) that contained the *programmable gates*, as well as a *programmable interconnect* between the CLBs.

Early FPGAs were usually used as glue logic between other fixed hardware components. However, the tremendous development of FPGAs in the 1990s, made FPGAs an attractive alternative to ASICs for prototyping, small volume production, for products with a short time to market, or products that require frequent modifications.

Today, FPGAs are enhanced with many additional hardware components that are integrated directly into the FPGA fabric such as embedded digital signal processing units (DSP), network cores, and even full-fledged processors, e.g., the ARM Cortex™-A9, which is embedded in the Xilinx Zynq™-7000 programmable SoC.

In summary, FPGAs have gone through an extreme evolution in the last three decades. Today, FPGAs provide massive parallelism, low power consumption, and high-speed I/O capabilities, which makes them interesting devices for data processing with compute- and data-intensive workloads.

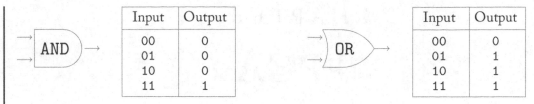

Figure 3.1: AND gate (left) and OR gate (right), each represented by a two-input LUT.

3.2   LOOK-UP TABLES—THE KEY TO RE-PROGRAMMABILITY

In Chapter 2, we saw that the three fundamental ingredients of any circuit are *combinational logic* (compute), *memory elements* (storage), and *interconnect* (communication). In the following, we will discuss these aspects in the context of FPGAs. In an ASIC, combinational logic is built from wiring a number of physical basic logic gates together. In FPGAs, these logic gates are simulated using multiple instances of a generic element called a *look-up table*—or simply LUT. As we will see, LUTs can be (re)programmed after manufacturing, which makes them mainly responsible for the (re)programmability property of FPGAs.

3.2.1   LUT REPRESENTATION OF A BOOLEAN FUNCTION

An n-input LUT can be used to implement an arbitrary Boolean-valued function with up to n Boolean arguments. Two simple examples of a two-input AND gate and a two-input OR gate, each implemented by a two-input LUT, are given in Figure 3.1.

3.2.2   INTERNAL ARCHITECTURE OF AN LUT

An n-input LUT requires 2^n bits of SRAM to store the lookup table, and a $2^n : 1$ multiplexer to read out a given configuration bit—typically implemented as a tree of $2 : 1$ multiplexers. 4-input LUTs used to be the standard, but today 6-input LUTs are more common. For readability, an example of a 4-input LUT is given in Figure 3.2.

As illustrated in the figure, the Boolean values at the inputs in_0 to in_3 determine which SRAM bit is forwarded to the output (*out*) of the LUT. The LUT in the illustration can be used to implement any 4-input Boolean expression. However, in practice, LUTs are even more sophisticated, e.g., the 4-input LUT above could also be used to implement two 3-input LUTs. Hence, typical LUTs today have not only one output port but several to support such configurations.

3.2.3   LUT (RE)PROGRAMMING

Since the configuration of an LUT, i.e., what Boolean function the LUT implements, is stored in SRAM, programming an LUT boils down to updating the SRAM cells of a given LUT. Inter-

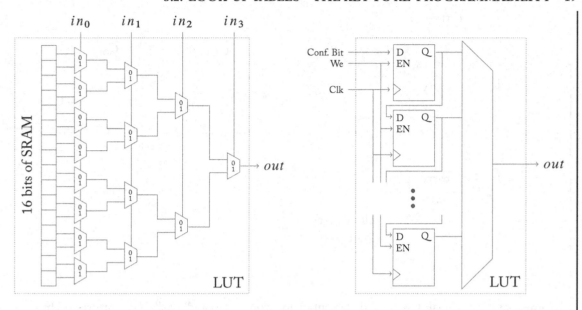

Figure 3.2: Internal structure of a 4-input LUT: circuitry for reading (left) and writing (right).

nally, these SRAM cells are organized as shift registers (1-bit wide and 2^n-bits deep), as depicted on the right of Figure 3.2. Thus, the bits of the configuration bitstream are shifted bit-by-bit into the LUTs when an FPGA is (re)programmed. Thus, an LUT can be read (asynchronously) in less than a cycle but writing to an LUT requires 2^n cycles. This reflects one of the typical trade-offs in hardware design—here, write performance is traded for a simpler design and, as a result, reduced chip space consumption.

3.2.4   ALTERNATIVE USAGE OF LUTS

So far, we have described how LUTs can be used to simulate gates, i.e., as combinational logic. However, since a key component of a LUT is SRAM, LUTs can also be used as *memory elements* of a circuit implemented on an FPGA.

When an FPGA is programmed, some LUTs can be configured to be used as so-called *distributed RAM*, i.e., a LUT can be configured as a small $n \times 1$ LUT RAM. Multiple LUT RAMs can then be combined with others for deeper and/or wider memories. Distributed RAM is a good choice for relatively small embedded RAM blocks within a circuit, e.g. to implement small FIFOs.

LUTs can also be configured to implement yet another fundamental memory element, namely as shift registers. As illustrated in Figure 3.2 (right), the shift register functionality is already present in the LUT as part of the write logic. Shift registers are useful, for example, to build delay lines to compensate for certain latencies of other circuit components.

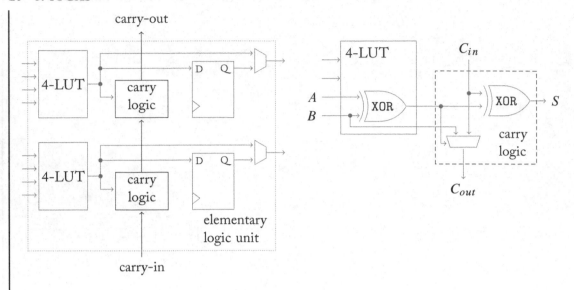

Figure 3.3: Functionality within an elementary logic unit (left) and a *full adder* constructed by combining a LUT with elements of the carry logic (right).

3.3   FPGA ARCHITECTURE

After discussing the key ideas behind look-up tables (LUTs) in the previous section, we now focus on how these LUTs are embedded into coarser architectural units and distributed across the FPGA fabric.

3.3.1   ELEMENTARY LOGIC UNITS (SLICES/ALMS)

A fixed number of LUTs are grouped and embedded into a programmable logic component, which we will call *elementary logic unit* (Xilinx refers to these units as *slices*, whereas Altera calls them *adaptive logic modules* (ALMs)). The exact architecture of *elementary logic units* varies among different vendors and even between different generations of FPGAs from the same vendor. Nevertheless, we can identify four main structural elements of an elementary logic unit: *(i)* a number of LUTs (typically between two and eight), *(ii)* a proportional number of 1-bit registers, *(iii)* arithmetic/carry logic, *(iv)* and several multiplexers.

An example elementary logic unit is illustrated in Figure 3.3, on the left-hand side. For presentation purposes, this elementary logic unit has only two 4-input LUTs with two corresponding flip-flop registers. This architecture can be considered classic (i.e., slices of Xilinx Virtex-4 and earlier FPGAs are based on this architecture) but modern FPGAs typically have more LUTs per elementary logic unit.

Each LUT is paired with a flip-flop, i.e., a 1-bit memory element to store the result of a table look-up. This facilitates pipelined circuit designs, where signals may propagate through large parts of the FPGA chip while a high clock frequency is maintained. Next to LUT-based memories these flip-flops are the second type of memory elements present in FPGAs. Whether a flip-flop is used or by-passed is determined by a multiplexer. The multiplexers in the elementary logic units can be driven by additional SRAM that is also set when an FPGA is programmed.

Finally, FPGAs have fast dedicated wires between neighboring LUTs and their corresponding circuitry. The most common type of such communication channels are *carry chains*. Carry chains allow combining multiple LUTs to implement arithmetic functions such as adders and multipliers. In Figure 3.3 (left), the blue path represents a carry chain (though somewhat simplified, e.g., wires to the flip-flop or output multiplexer have been omitted).

Typically, the vertical wires of the carry chain pass through dedicated carry logic that helps in the construction of particular arithmetic functions. For example, on the right-hand side of Figure 3.3, a *full adder* (1-bit adder) is constructed using an XOR gate (implemented by the LUT) together with another XOR gate, as well as a 2-to-1 multiplexer of the carry logic. Via the vertical carry wires a cascade of such full adders can be used to create wider adders.

3.4   ROUTING ARCHITECTURE

Direct wires to neighboring *elementary logic units* (e.g., carry chains) allow combining multiple units to build more sophisticated circuits such as adders and multipliers. However, modern FPGAs provide enough configurable resources to host an entire *system on chip* (SoC). But to build such a complex system a more flexible communication mechanism is required to connect different sub-circuits spread out over the FPGA fabric. This communication mechanism is known as the *interconnect*.

3.4.1   LOGIC ISLANDS

A small number of *elementary logic units* (cf. Section 3.3.1) are grouped together into a coarser grained unit that we refer to as *logic island* (corresponding to *configurable logic blocks* (CLBs) or *logic array blocks* (LBAs) in the terminology of Xilinx and Altera, respectively). An example, resembling the CLBs of Virtex-5 and Virtex-6 FPGAs, is given in Figure 3.4, on the left-hand side.

In this example, a logic island consists of two elementary logic units. Each elementary logic unit has a separate set of wires (e.g., for carry-chains, etc.) running vertically through the chip and connecting elementary logic units of adjacent logic islands. For more general communication among logic islands the elementary logic units of every logic island are connected to the interconnect via *switch matrix*, which we will discuss in just a moment.

On the right-hand side of Figure 3.4, we show how the logic islands are arranged as a two-dimensional array on the FPGA. The flexible interconnect between the logic islands allows for arbitrary communication patterns, say, LI_{00} could be talking to LI_{21}, which is three hops (wiring

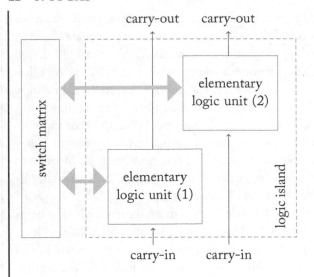
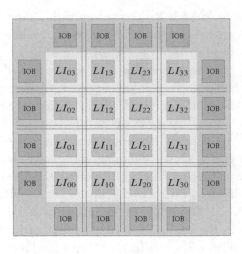

Figure 3.4: Internals of a *logic island* (left) and two-dimensional arrangement of *logic islands* ($LI_{xy}s$) on an FPGA (right), surrounded by I/O blocks (IOBs).

segments) away. The interconnect also makes it possible for logic islands to directly communicate with special I/O blocks (IOBs) located at the periphery of the FPGA (see Section 3.5).

3.4.2   INTERCONNECT

The *interconnect* is a configurable routing architecture that allows communication between arbitrary logic islands. It consists of communication channels (bundles of wires) that run horizontally and vertically across the chip, forming a grid containing a logic island in every grid cell.

As illustrated in Figure 3.5, at the intersection points of the routing channels there are *programmable links* that determine how the wires are connected, allowing to connect the outputs and the inputs of arbitrary logic islands or I/O blocks.

Each wire can be connected to any of the other three wires that come together at the intersection point, i.e., all those physical connections exist but programmable switches determine which connections are active. In the example, in Figure 3.5, a vertical connection (red) was programmed by setting the SRAM cell of the corresponding switch appropriately. Hence, wires can be programmed to take left or right turns or continue straight.

3.5   HIGH-SPEED I/O

As mentioned in the previous section, the two-dimensional array of logic islands is surrounded by a large amount of I/O blocks (IOBs). These IOBs sit at the periphery of the FPGA and are also

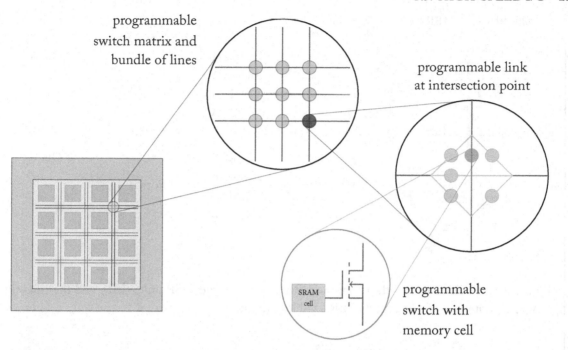

Figure 3.5: Routing architecture with *switch matrix*, *programmable links* at intersection points, and *programmable switches*.

connected to the programmable interconnect, allowing the logic islands to communicate with the outside world (cf. Figure 3.4).

Also the IOBs can be programmed to serve different needs and allow the FPGA to communicate with a multitude of other devices. Typically, many I/O standards are supported, with the two main classes of I/O standards being *single-ended* (used, e.g., in PCI) and for higher performance *differential* (used, e.g., in PCI Express, SATA, 10G Ethernet, etc.). Typically, the IOBs also contain certain auxiliary hardware such as serial-to-parallel converters or 8b/10b encoders/decoders that are used in a number of communication protocols. In a nutshell, the IOBs can be programmed to implement the *physical layer* of many common communication schemes.

High-speed (multi-gigabit) I/O is implemented using extremely fast serial transceivers[1] at the heart of the IOBs. The fastest transceivers, at the time of writing this book, are the GTH/GTZ type transceivers of the Virtex-7 HT FPGAs from Xilinx, providing 28 Gb/s serial bandwidth each—by comparison, SATA Gen 3 requires 6 Gb/s serial bandwidth. The Virtex-7 HT FPGA ships with sixteen 28 Gb/s and seventy-two 13 Gb/s transceivers. Thus, aggregate bandwidth of more than a terabit per second can be achieved with these FPGAs.

---

[1]A transceiver is an electronic device consisting of both a *trans*mitter and a re*ceiver*.

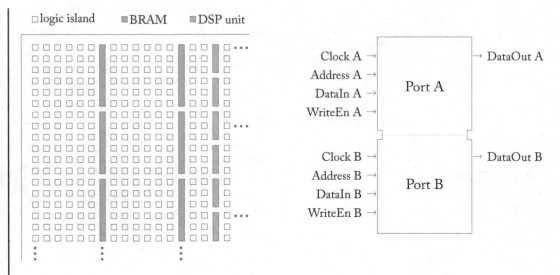

Figure 3.6: FPGA layout with interspersed BRAM blocks and DSP units (left), and the (slightly simplified) interface of a dual-ported BRAM block (right).

3.6 AUXILIARY ON-CHIP COMPONENTS

The logic resources of FPGAs discussed so far are in principle sufficient to implement a wide range of circuits. However, to address high-performance and usability needs of some applications, FPGA vendors additionally intersperse FPGAs with special silicon components (cf. Figure 3.6) such as dedicated RAM blocks (BRAM), multipliers and adders (DSP units), and in some cases even full-fledged CPU cores. Hence, Herbordt et al. [2008] observed that the model for FPGAs has evolved from a "bag of gates" to a "bag of computer parts."

3.6.1 BLOCK RAM (BRAM)

On the left-hand side of Figure 3.6, a common layout of the different components within an FPGA is illustrated. Between the columns of logic islands there are columns of dedicated RAM blocks typically referred to as *Block RAM* (BRAM). A single BRAM block can hold a few kilobytes of data (e.g., 4 KiB), and usually an FPGA holds a few hundred BRAMs, which can all be accessed in parallel. BRAM access is very fast, i.e., a word can be read or written in a single clock cycle at a clock speed of several hundred megahertz.

Compared to *distributed RAM*, discussed in Section 3.2.4, BRAMs provide significantly higher density but can only be instantiated at a coarser grain, making them the ideal choice to store larger working set data on-chip. As with distributed RAM, multiple BRAMs can be combined to form larger memories.

On Virtex FPGAs, BRAMs are dual-ported, as depicted on the right-hand side of Figure 3.6. This means that the BRAM can be accessed concurrently by two different circuits. The word width for each port is configurable, i.e., one circuit might choose to access BRAM at a byte granularity, while another addresses BRAM in four-byte chunks. Each port is driven by a separate clock, i.e., the two circuits accessing the BRAM may run at different speeds. Furthermore, a dual-ported BRAM can be configured to behave as two single-ported BRAMs (each one-half the original size) or even as FIFO-queues.

BRAMs can be used for clock domain crossing and bus width conversion in an elegant way. For instance, an Ethernet circuit clocked at 125 MHz could directly write data of received packets into a BRAM, configured as a FIFO buffer, one byte at a time. On the other side, a consuming circuit with a different clock speed, say 200 MHz, could choose to read from that same buffer at a 4-byte granularity.

3.6.2 DIGITAL SIGNAL PROCESSING (DSP) UNITS

FPGAs are attractive for digital signal processing (*e.g*, digital filtering, Fourier analysis, etc.), which heavily relies on mathematical operations. However, while adders and multipliers can be built from the LUTs and flip-flops provided in an FPGA, they can by no means compete—in terms of performance, space, and power consuption—with corresponding circuits in pure silicon. Therefore, FPGA manufacturers also embed dedicated hardware multipliers and adders (between less than a hundred to a few thousand) in their FPGAs. A *finite impulse response* (FIR) filter is a typical DSP application. An example of a FIR filter is given below:

$$y[n] = a_0 x[n] + a_1 x[n-1] + a_2 x[n-2]$$

(where $x[n]/y[n]$ indicate the filter's input/output values at clock cycle n, respectively).

This filter processes a stream of input samples in a "sliding window" manner, i.e., the last three input samples are multiplied by some coefficients (a_0, a_1, a_2) and then accumulated. A typical (fully pipelined) hardware implementation of such as filter is depicted in Figure 3.7. All three multiplications and additions are computed in parallel and intermediate results are stored in flip-flop registers (▮). Because this combination of *multiply and accumulate* (MAC) is so frequently used in DSP applications, a DSP unit, in essence, usually comprises a multiplier and an adder.

As with most other components in FPGAs, the DSP units can also be customized and combined with adjacent DSP units. For example, a Xilinx DSP48E slice has three input ports (which are 25 bits, 18 bits, 48 bits wide) and provides a 25×18-bit multiplier in combination with a pipelined *second stage* that can be programmed as 48-bit subtractor or adder with optional accumulation feedback. Hence, these DSP units can be used in a variety of modes, and perform operations such as multiply, multiply-and-accumulate, multiply-and-add/subtract, three input addition, wide bus multiplexing, barrel shifting, etc., on wide inputs in only one or two clock cycles. In the database context, fast multipliers are very useful, e.g., to implement efficient hash functions.

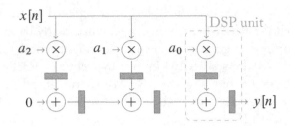

Figure 3.7: Fully pipelined FIR filter constructed from three DSP units.

3.6.3   SOFT AND HARD IP-CORES

FPGAs are a great tool to create custom hardware but development effort is still significantly higher than for writing software. Certain functionality is fairly standardized and used in many FPGA designs over and over again. Thus, so-called *intellectual property* (IP) cores can be instantiated in FPGA designs. In essence, an IP core is a reusable unit of logic—free or commercial—ranging from circuits for simple arithmetic operations to entire microprocessors. A *soft* IP core implements the corresponding functionality using standard programmable resources provided by the FPGA, while a *hard* IP core refers to a dedicated silicon component embedded in the FPGA fabric.

BRAMs and DSP units are the simplest form of embedded silicon components on FPGAs. Often FPGA vendors also add more complex hard-wired circuitry to their FPGAs to support common functionality at high performance with minimal chip space consumption. A typical example is the *medium access controller* (MAC) core found on many FPGAs, connected to an Ethernet PHY device[2] on the corresponding FPGA card, providing high-level access to Ethernet frames.

Some FPGAs even incorporate full-fledged hard CPU cores. Several older generations of Xilinx's Virtex FPGAs shipped with embedded PowerPC cores, e.g., the Virtex-5 FX130T integrates two PowerPC 440 cores (800 MHz). FPGAs of the newer Xilinx Zynq series include an ARM Cortex-A9 dual-core (1 GHz). Also Altera produces FPGAs with embedded ARM cores, and Intel in collaboration with Altera designed an embedded processor (Stellarton) that combines an Atom core with an FPGA in the same package.[3]

3.7   FPGA PROGRAMMING

Having discussed the key ingredients of FPGAs, we now take a closer look at how FPGAs are programmed. From a high-level perspective, the FPGA design flow is very similar to generating hard-wired circuits, which we discussed in the previous chapter (Section 2.3). It's the tools pro-

---

[2]The PHY connects Ethernet circuitry to a physical medium such as optical fiber or copper cable.
[3]Please note that here the Atom processor and the FPGA communicate via PCI Express, i.e., this is more of a system-in-package than a true system on chip (SoC).

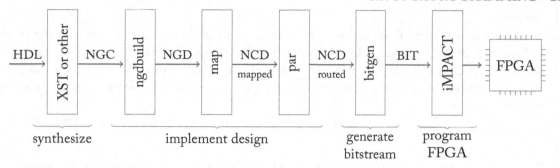

Figure 3.8: FPGA design flow: Xilinx tool chain and intermediate circuit specification formats.

vided by the FPGA vendors that do all the magic of mapping a generic circuit specification onto FPGA hardware.

3.7.1 FPGA DESIGN FLOW

To illustrate a typical FPGA design flow, we will examine the tools of the Xilinx tool chain, as well as their intermediate circuit representations. For some of the terminology used in this section, we refer to Chapter 2, where we discussed fundamental hardware design concepts. The most important steps and tools of the design flow to produce an FPGA-circuit are depicted in Figure 3.8.

Synthesis

The entry point to programming FPGAs is the same as for producing hard-wired circuits, i.e., typically by using a hardware description language (HDL) such as VHDL or Verilog. The Xilinx synthesizer (XST) turns an HDL specification into a collection of gate-level netlists (*native generic circuit* (NGC) format), mapped to a technology library (UNISIM) provided by Xilinx. However, at this level also third-party synthesizers (e.g., Synplicity) may be used, which typically store the netlist using an industry-standard EDIF[4] format.

Translate

The tool **ngdbuild** combines and *translates* all input netlists and *constraints* into a single netlist saved as *native generic database* (NGD) file. The FPGA designer specifies constraints in a so-called *user constraint file* (UCF). Constraints are used to assign special physical elements of the FPGA (e.g., I/O pins, clocks, etc.) to ports of modules in the design, as well as to specify timing requirements of the design. Whereas the NGC netlist is based on the UNISIM library for *behavioral* simulation, the NGD netlist is based on the SIMPRIM library, which also allows *timing* simulation.

---

[4]EDIF stands for electronic design interchange format.

Map

The **map** tool *maps* the SIMPRIM primitives in an NGD netlist to specific device resources such as logic islands, I/O blocks, BRAM blocks, etc. The **map** tool then generates a *native circuit description* (NCD) file that describes the circuit, now mapped to physical FPGA components. Notice that this is an additional step not needed in the classical design flow for generating circuits (cf. Section 2.3).

Place and Route

Placement and routing is performed by the **par** tool. The physical elements specified in the NCD file are placed at precise locations on the FPGA chip and *interconnected*. While doing so, **par** takes *timing constraints* specified in the user constraint file (UCF) into account. Oftentimes, place and route (based on simulated annealing algorithms) is the most time consuming step in the design flow, and multiple iterations may be necessary to comply with all timing constraints. The **par** tool takes the *mapped* NCD file and generates a *routed* NCD file, which also contains the routing information.

Bitstream Generation and Device Programming

Now the routed design needs to be loaded onto the FPGA. However, the design must first be converted into an FPGA-readable format. This is handled by the **bitgen** tool, which encodes the design into a binary, known as *bitstream*. The bitstream can then be loaded onto the FPGA, e.g., via JTAG cable and using the **iMPACT** tool. As a side note, modern FPGAs often also feature the possibility to *encrypt* and *authenticate* bitstreams to support security-sensitive applications.

The bitstream controls a finite state machine inside the FPGA, which extracts configuration data from the bitstream and block-wise loads it into the FPGA chip. Xilinx calls these blocks *frames*. Each frame is stored in a designated location in the configuration SRAM that directly relates to a physical site on the FPGA (cf. Figure 3.9) and configures the various configurable elements on that site, e.g., multiplexers, inverters, different types of LUTs, and other configuration parameters. Once the configuration memory is completely written, the FPGA is *programmed* and ready for operation.

3.7.2 DYNAMIC PARTIAL RECONFIGURATION

As noted in the previous section, configuration memory of an FPGA is divided into *frames*, of which each corresponds to a specific physical site on the FPGA. These frames are the smallest addressable units of device configuration and are distributed across the FPGA, as illustrated on the left-hand side of Figure 3.9. A frame always groups together a column of elementary blocks of some type such as logic islands, BRAM blocks, I/O blocks, etc. In earlier FPGAs (e.g., Xilinx Virtex-2 FPGAs), a frame would span the entire hight of the FPGA chip but nowadays frames are usually arranged in multiple rows. To give an idea of the granularity of these configuration frames,

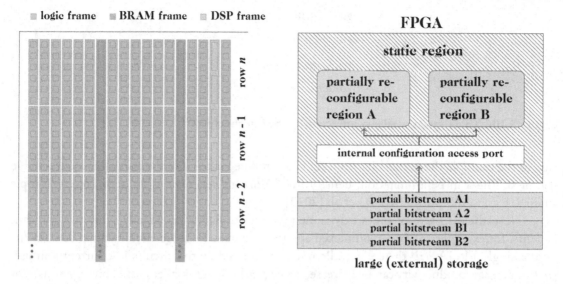

Figure 3.9: Configuration regions of an FPGA, comprising multiple elementary blocks of one type, covered by *configuration frames* (left), and an FPGA programmed with two *partially reconfigurable regions* (PRRs) and corresponding partial bitstreams stored externally (right).

in Virtex-4, Virtex-5, and Virtex-6 FPGAs a CLB-frame (i.e., for logic island configuration) spans 16×1, 20×1, and 40×1 CLBs, respectively.

The organization of configuration memory described above is the basis for a technique known as *dynamic partial reconfiguration*. This technique allows parts of an FPGA to be reprogrammed without interrupting other *running* parts on the same FPGA. To do so, only the frames of a particular *partial reconfiguration region* (PRR) are updated with a new configuration, while the other frames are left unchanged.

Dynamic partial reconfiguration enables interesting applications, where specialized modules can be loaded on-demand at run time without occupying precious chip space when they are inactive. To load a hardware module, a control unit on the FPGA (e.g., a processor) loads configuration data from some external source—for example, from off-chip DRAM—and sends it to the so-called *Internal Configuration Access Port* (ICAP),[5] which is the gateway to the configuration memory of the FPGA.

The above scenario is illustrated on the right-hand side of Figure 3.9. Notice that fixed *partially reconfigurable regions* (PRRs) need to be defined beforehand, i.e., when the static part of a circuit is designed. Those regions then serve as placeholders, into which a bitstream can be loaded later on. A *partial bitstream* can be only loaded into the exact PRR that it was designed for,

---

[5]Note that Xilinx has a longer history of supporting dynamic partial reconfiguration in their FPGAs than Altera, which is why in this section we use Xilinx-specific terminology and focus on the design flow for Xilinx devices.

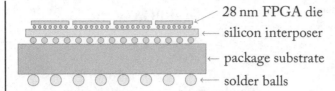

Figure 3.10: Xilinx's stacked silicon interconnect (SSI) technology.

e.g., in the example the partial bitstream A1 could not be loaded into the partially reconfigurable region B. This can be a limitation, hence *partial bitstream relocation* is an active research topic studied, e.g., in the work of Touiza et al. [2012].

Nevertheless, state-of-the-art dynamic partial reconfiguration already exhibits significant benefits, for example: *(i)* time-multiplexed applications may use more circuitry than actually fits onto a single FPGA, *(ii)* there is no idle power consumed by the circuits not currently in use, *(iii)* and design productivity can be increased since synthesizing smaller partial bitstreams is a lot faster than full bitstreams synthesis.

3.8   ADVANCED TECHNOLOGY AND FUTURE TRENDS

After having discussed established core FPGA technology, in this section, we look into what is currently happening at the forefront of FPGA research and innovation. We selected a few topics ranging from FPGA manufacturing and FPGA architecture to how FPGAs could be programmed in the future.

3.8.1   DIE STACKING

FPGAs have a long history of being at the leading edge of semiconductor technology innovation. As such, Xilinx produced one of the first devices that introduced so-called *die stacking*—the Virtex-7 2000T. Die stacking (also referred to as 3D ICs) is a technique to assemble and combine multiple dies within the same package. The difference to assembling multiple chips on a *printed circuit board* (PCB) is that the dies can be assembled at the same density as a monolithic solution, leading to better performance and less power consumption.

The problem with large monolithic FPGAs is that at the early stages of a new manufacturing process (shrinking transistors), there are many defective dies. In fact, die yield dramatically decreases as a function of die size. Therefore very large monolithic FPGAs are typically only manufactured once the process matures. Thus, one benefit of die stacking is that large FPGAs can be produced early on. The Virtex-7 2000T that was released in 2011 consisted of 6.8 billion transistors, making it the largest FPGA ever.

Figure 3.10 illustrates Xilinx's stacked silicon interconnect (SSI) technology used for the Virtex-7 2000T. Four FPGA dies, fabricated using a 28 nm manufacturing process, are soldered side by side on top of the so-called *silicon interposer*.[6] The interposer is a *passive* silicon chip that connects adjacent FPGA dies via tens of thousands of connections, allowing for very high bandwidth, low latency, and low power consumption. Note that side by side stacking avoids a number of thermal issues that could result from stacking multiple FPGA dies on top of each other.

3.8.2   HETEROGENEOUS DIE-STACKED FPGAS

The Virtex-7 2000T, discussed in the previous section, can be thought of as homogeneous since the four dies are all identical FPGA dies. In 2012, Xilinx took its die stacking technology one step further and introduced the Virtex-7 H580T, which assembles *heterogeneous* dies in the same package. In particular, the Virtex-7 H580T combines two FPGA dies with one transceiver die, that hosts multiple 28 Gb/s transceivers. Thus, the analog portions of the transceivers are physically separated from the digital portions of the FPGA, isolating the transceivers from noise and ensuring very high signal integrity.

At the broader scale, heterogeneous die stacking is about integrating different process technologies into the same package. *Logic*, *analog*, and *memory* (DRAM) chips have very different optimization constraints, and are thus produced independently. Integrating these technologies on the same die would be feasible but not economical. Notice that integrating, for example, a CPU core into an FPGA die is not as problematic because CPUs and FPGAs are both logic and use the same process technology. Fortunately, heterogeneous die stacking allows integrating dies produced using different process technologies into the same package in an economically sensible way. In the future, die stacking might bring several new interesting FPGAs, as for example, FPGAs with integrated DRAM memory.

3.8.3   TIME-MULTIPLEXED FPGAS

Tabula is a semiconductor start-up that introduced a fundamentally new FPGA architecture with their ABAX product family, in 2010. Existing FPGA architectures suffer from the fact that an increasing amount of die area is used for the interconnect rather than logic elements, as process technology shrinks. In other words, there would be enough space on the silicon for more logic elements, but interconnecting them is the problem.

To avoid this underutilization of chip space, Tabula replicates FPGA resources (e.g., LUTs, flip-flops, multiplexers, and interconnect) eight times and then switches between those independent sets of resources—so-called "folds"—at a very high frequency (1.6 GHz). In a sense, eight smaller FPGAs execute in a time-multiplexed manner, and simulate a larger FPGA, where each individual fold runs with a clock period of 625 picoseconds, resulting in an overall clock period of 5 nanoseconds.

---

[6]Xilinx refers to SSI as being a 2.5D technology. What is meant is that active silicon (FPGA dies) are mounted on passive silicon (the interposer). By contrast, 3D die stacking refers to active-on-active stacking, *e.g*, multiple FPGAs on top of each other, which might be supported in future devices.

Tabula refers to this concept as "3-dimensional chips" of eight folds, where logic elements not only connect to adjacent logic elements in the two-dimensional space, as in traditional FPGA architectures, but also to logic cells in the "above" fold. This is made possible using "transparent latches" in the interconnect, which are controlled by time-multiplexing circuitry, and allow communication between different folds.

The ABAX chip can be programmed exactly the same way as one would program a commodity FPGA, i.e., the high-speed reconfiguration and time-multiplexing is completely hidden from the programmer. The key advantage of this technology is that it can provide the same amount of logic resources as large commodity FPGAs, however, at a significantly lower price, i.e., in the range of 100-200 USD. Hence, the technology is very promising. As a result, Tabula was ranked third on the Wall Street's Journal's annual "Next Big Thing" list in 2012 [Basich and Maltby, 2012].

3.8.4   HIGH-LEVEL SYNTHESIS

As FPGA technology is developing at a rapid pace, producing chips with an ever increasing number of programmable resources, the evolution of programming paradigms for FPGAs has been lagging far behind, i.e., the de facto standard for many years has been to write code at the RTL level (see Section 2.3.1) using a hardware description language such as VHDL or Verilog. Programming at this level of abstraction is difficult and error-prone, leading to long design cycles and a steep learning curve for developers coming from the software world, which is hindering the wide-spread adoption of FPGA technology.

To make FPGAs accessible to a wider range of developers and to lower time to market, there have been significant research efforts to enable the translation of higher-level languages into hardware circuits—so-called *high-level synthesis* (HLS) or *electronic system level* (ESL) synthesis. Xilinx's new design suite *Vivado*, for example, supports synthesizing C-based algorithmic circuit specifications. The actual HLS tool is based on *Autopilot* from *AutoESL*, a high-level synthesis vendor that Xilinx purchased in 2011.

By contrast, Altera is pushing for high-level synthesis based on *OpenCL*, which is a framework for writing parallel programs that execute across a number of different platforms such as multicore CPUs and GPUs. OpenCL is well known for *general purpose GPU* (GPGPU) programming, where serial routines on the CPU control a heavy parallel workload that is executed on the GPU. In OpenCL so-called *kernels* that execute on OpenCL devices, e.g., a GPU, are specified using the C-based OpenCL language. Whereas a GPU executes such kernels on fixed compute cores, in an FPGA, the compute cores are highly customizable, and it is expected that often similar performance to that of GPUs can be achieved, however, with significantly lower energy consumption. While a HLS compiler makes it easier to specify hardware circuits, testing the generated circuits is still cumbersome. Since OpenCL is not just a language and a compiler but also includes an execution framework, it has the potential to eventually also make testing and debugging more productive.

CHAPTER 4

FPGA Programming Models

We mainly looked at FPGAs from the hardware technology side so far. Clearly, the use and "programming" of FPGAs is considerably different to the programming models that software developers are used to. In this chapter, we will show how entire system designs can be derived from a given application context, and we will show how those designs can be made to benefit from the intrinsic properties of FPGA hardware (or how work can be partitioned, so solutions can get the most out of hard- and software).

We will start the chapter (Section 4.1) with a discussion about trade-offs in flexibility and performance and how one can avoid very high circuit compilation cost. In Section 4.2, we show how a given application problem can actually be turned into a hardware circuit. In Sections 4.3 and 4.4 we then illustrate how generated circuits can be optimized by leveraging *data* and *pipeline parallelism* (respectively).

4.1 RE-BUILD, PARAMETERIZE, OR PROGRAM THE HARDWARE ACCELERATOR?

FPGAs provide the opportunity to modify and re-configure the FPGA at a very fine granularity, even from one user query to the next. We will, in fact, discuss some systems that follow this route later in Chapter 5. The strategy is not appropriate for all application scenarios, however. The problem is that circuit (re-)compilation is an extremely CPU-intensive operation. Necessary steps, such as component placement and routing are highly compute-intensive, and they scale poorly with the circuit size. In practice, several minutes of compilation are the norm; some circuits might require hours to be generated.

On the positive side, circuit re-building has the potential to generate highly efficient (if not "optimal") circuits for a very wide range of problem instances. Effectively, system designers face three design goals:

(a) Runtime Performance. At runtime, the hardware solution should have good performance characteristics. Ideally, these characteristics should be close to those of a hand-crafted, tailor-made circuit for the problem instance at hand.

(b) Flexibility/Expressiveness. The solution should support a wide range of problem instances. SQL, for instance, is expressive enough to cover many useful applications.

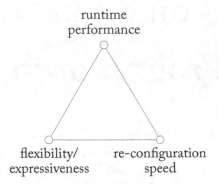

Figure 4.1: Design space for FPGA programming model. Design goals are execution performance at runtime; flexibility/expressiveness to support different problem instances; and a fast way to realize workload changes. Not all goals can be maximized at the same time.

(c) Re-Configuration Speed. When workloads change, the hardware solution should be able to react to such changes with low latency. To illustrate, having to wait for minute- or hour-long circuit routing is certainly inappropriate for ad hoc query processing.

Unfortunately, not all of these goals can be reached at the same time. Rather, designers have to make compromises between the opposing goals. As illustrated with Figure 4.1, at most two goals can be met satisfactory—at the expense of the third.

4.1.1 RE-BUILDING CIRCUITS AT RUNTIME

Circuit re-compilation enables optimizing runtime performance and expressiveness, but sacrifices re-configuration speed. It could thus be placed in the design space as shown here on the right.

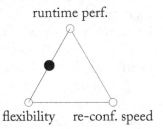

Because of the high re-configuration effort, the model seems most appropriate whenever the workload is mostly static and long re-compilation times are acceptable.[1] Examples could be risk management for electronic trading systems (we shall see one example in Section 5.3.1) or network intrusion detection (Section 5.1.4), where rule sets to match change only at a longer time scale.

Pre-Compiled Modules, Partial Reconfiguration
The re-compilation effort can be reduced through the use of pre-compiled modules that the circuit generator merely stitches together to obtain a working hardware solution for a given problem

---

[1]Note that circuit re-compilation is a software-only task. The FPGA must be taken off-line only to upload the compiled bitstream. This time is relatively short and technology exists to eliminate it altogether (using multi-context FPGAs).

instance. The system of Dennl et al. [2012], for instance, includes modules for relational algebra operators that can be used to construct a physical representation of an algebraic query plan on the two-dimensional chip space.

Pre-compiled modules work well together with *partial re-configuration*, selective replacement of only some areas on the FPGA chip (cf. Section 3.7.2). And when these areas are small, also less time is needed to move the (partial) bitstream to the device, which may further improve responsiveness to workload changes.

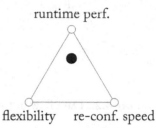

Only so much variety can be pre-compiled, however, which limits the flexibility that can be achieved by following this route. In our three-goal design space, this moves the approach toward faster re-configuration speed, but at the expense of flexibility (illustrated on the right). Pre-compiled modules and partial re-configuration can also be combined with parameterization to improve the flexibility/performance trade-off. We will look at this technique in a moment.

At this point we would like to mention that circuit re-construction is not only compute-intensive. It also implies that, at application runtime, a stack of hardware design tools has to be executed for synthesis, placement/routing, and bitstream generation. Installation, maintenance, and licensing of these tools might be too complex and expensive to employ the approach in practical settings. If used with partial re-configuration, pre-compiled modules might not actually depend on the availability of these tools. But partial re-configuration has yet to prove its maturity practical use. Most commercial users would likely refrain from using the technology today in real-world settings.

4.1.2 PARAMETERIZED CIRCUITS

Commercial uses of FPGAs often do not re-generate circuits after system deployment at all and treat them similarly to a hard-wired ASIC. Hardware re-configurability is used here only to *(a)* perform occasional hardware/software updates and *(b)* avoid the high production cost of ASICs when the application's market size is too small. Adaptation to application workloads is then achieved via *parameterization*. The idea is that the hardware circuit itself is hard-wired, but at runtime it reads out and interprets a number of configuration parameters that describe the current workload.

For certain workloads, this model is a good fit. If, for instance, the FPGA is used only to filter a tuple stream based on a simple predicate, say

$$column\text{-}name \; \theta \; constant$$

(where θ is some comparison operator $=, <, \leq, \dots$), then *column-name*, θ, and *constant* can be left as a configuration parameter in an otherwise hard-wired circuit.

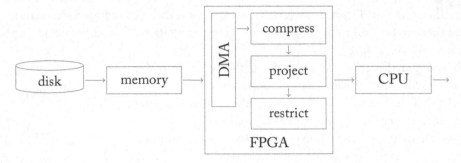

Figure 4.2: Data flow in the Netezza FAST engine (adapted from Francisco [2011]).

An example of this model is the Netezza Data Appliance Architecture. The included *FAST engine* ("FPGA-accelerated streaming technology") uses a fixed processing pipeline to perform data preprocessing in FPGA hardware. This pipeline, illustrated in Figure 4.2, first decompresses the raw table data, then performs projection and row selection in sequence. Not shown in the figure is a "visibility engine" that discards tuples not valid for the current transaction (e.g., uncommitted data).

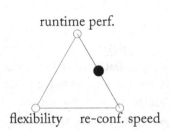

Through runtime parameters, the FAST engine can be configured to run most of the critical tasks in the application areas that Netezza was designed for. Parameter updates can be applied almost instantaneously, since the necessary amount of configuration is very small. But the engine cannot be configured beyond this well-defined query pattern. In terms of our design space illustration, Netezza offers good runtime performance and fast re-configuration. But it gives up flexibility, compared to systems that employ circuit re-construction, as illustrated here on the left.

Example: Skeleton Automata

Parameterization can actually be quite powerful. Its potential reaches far beyond only the setting of selection parameters or column names. The approach is expressive enough to cover a large and, most importantly, relevant subset of *XPath*, the de facto standard to access XML data [Teubner et al., 2012]. Pushing this subset to an accelerator may speed up, e.g., an in-memory XQuery processor by large factors.

XPath can be implemented with help of finite-state automata, driven by the sequence of opening and closing tags in the XML input. The structure of these automata depends on the user query. The relevant insight now is that the class of automata that can arise is constrained by the XPath language specification. This constraint is sufficient to build a "skeleton automaton" that includes any transition edge that could be expressed with XPath. By making the condition assigned to each of these edges a configuration parameter, the skeleton automaton can be parameterized

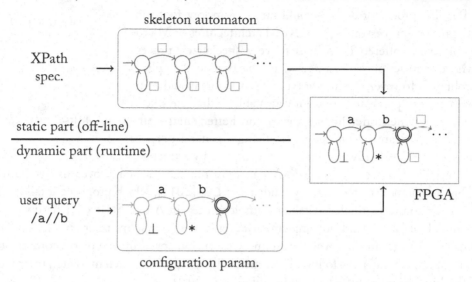

Figure 4.3: Parameterization offers excellent runtime and re-configuration performance, but limits the expressiveness addressable by the hardware accelerator. "Skeleton automata" illustrate how a meaningful class of queries can be supported nevertheless. Edges of a general-purpose state automaton (the "skeleton automaton") can be parameterized to describe any relevant query automaton.

to run any XPath query (within the relevant dialect) as a true hardware NFA. Transitions not needed for a particular query can be assigned a 'false' condition parameter, effectively removing the transition from the automaton.

Figure 4.3 illustrates this concept. The skeleton automaton is generated based on the language semantics of XPath and uploaded to the FPGA once. The user query is then used to infer configuration parameters (printed blue in Figure 4.3), which are used to fill placeholders (indicated as □ in Figure 4.3) in the hardware circuit. Configuration parameters can be inferred and installed in a micro-second time scale, which guarantees full ad hoc query capabilities.

4.1.3 INSTRUCTION SET PROCESSORS ON TOP OF FPGAS

The remaining corner in our design space (see figure on the right below) is easy to fill. An *instruction set processor*, realized in the FPGA fabric, offers high flexibility and can be re-configured by merely changing the program it executes.

Possible processor designs could range from low-footprint general-purpose processors (such as ARM architectures or Micro-Blaze soft cores offered by Xilinx) to very specialized processors whose instruction set is targeted to the particular application problem. However, the former type of processors would compete with counterparts that are readily available as discrete silicon components—which offer higher speeds and better energy efficiency at a significantly lower price. Realizing a general-purpose processor on FPGA hardware alone thus seems hardly attractive.

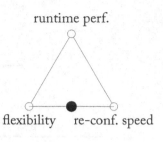

Specialized processors on FPGA hardware *can* have an edge over mainstream processors. This was demonstrated, e.g., by Vaidya and Lee [2011], which proposed a tailor-made co-processor for column-oriented databases, implemented in Altera Stratix III hardware. Though Vaidya and Lee [2011] did not implement an end-to-end system, their simulations indicated that this can lead to an improvement in query execution speed by one or two orders of magnitude. The approach had been followed commercially by Kickfire, which marketed their accelerator as "SQL chip." Kickfire was acquired by Teradata in 2010.

Mixed Designs.   The approaches listed above do not exclude one another. In fact, the potential of configurable hardware lies in the possibility to build hybrid designs. For instance, a hardware design could include a highly specialized, tailor-made circuit; fast, but only suited to run the most common case. The tailor-made circuit could be backed up by an instruction set processor that captures all remaining situations, such as infrequent request types, system setup, or exception handling. If these situations are rare, processor speed will not really matter to the overall system performance.

Commercially available FPGA hardware increasingly supports such mixed designs. In various forms, vendors offer FPGA chips where a general-purpose CPU is readily integrated as a discrete silicon component. This eases system design, reduces cost (since the instruction set processor does not occupy precious configurable chip space), and improves performance (discrete silicon blocks sustain higher clock frequencies). An example of such hardware is the Xilinx Zynq product line, which integrates a hard ARM core with configurable chip space.

4.2   FROM ALGORITHM TO CIRCUIT

The true potential of FPGA technology lies, of course, in the ability to create tailor-made circuits for a given application problem. But how can such circuit be inferred from a problem specification?

4.2.1   EXPRESSION → CIRCUIT

As discussed in the hardware design part of this book, any logic circuit consists of *combinational logic* and some form of *memory*. Both parts are glued together through a *wiring* that connects all parts of a circuit. Combinational logic can describe operations where the output only depends on the present operator input, but not on, e.g., previously seen input items. That is, combinational circuits describe *pure functions*. Combinational circuits can be wired up into larger combinational circuits simply according to the data flow of the functions that they describe. The operation

$$y = f\big(g(x_1), h(x_2)\big)$$

could thus be implemented as the circuit

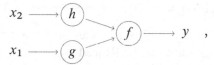

where $\boxed{f}$ indicates the sub-circuit that implements f. By construction, this leads to *directed acyclic graphs/circuits*.

Some application problems require access to previous values from the input and/or from the output. If we use $x[k]$ to denote the value of an (input) item x at clock cycle k, the two examples

$$y[k] = \frac{x[k-1] + x[k]}{2} \qquad \text{(Avg)} \qquad\qquad y[k] = y[k-1] + x[k] \qquad \text{(Sum)}$$

would access values from the preceding clock cycle to compute the average value of the last two x seen and the running sum of all x, respectively.

To implement such behavior, memory elements—flip-flop registers in practice—must be inserted into the data path(s) of the circuit. A register, indicated as rectangles ▌ as before, briefly stores the value that it receives at its input and makes it available on its output during the *next clock cycle*. The above two examples can then be expressed in hardware as follows:

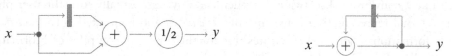

Observe how, in both cases, registers *delay* values by one clock cycles. To access even older items, multiple delay registers can be used one after another.

4.2.2   CIRCUIT GENERATION

Oftentimes, programmers need not explicitly draw circuit diagrams to turn an application problem into a hardware circuit. Rather, expressions that describe the combinational parts of a circuit can be phrased directly in a hardware description language (VHDL or Verilog). Modern design tools will then not only compose circuits automatically as illustrated above. They will also perform cross-operator optimizations, generally improving area and/or speed efficiency of the generated circuit.[2]

---

[2]For instance, in the Avg example, addition and division can be combined, simply by discarding any logic that would compute the least-significant bit of the + output.

For functions that require delay functionality, the circuit must be explicitly synchronized to a clock signal in the VHDL/Verilog code. If a (sub-)result must be carried from one clock cycle to the next (i.e., delayed) that result must explicitly be assigned to a register variable or signal. Design tools will, however, try to eliminate redundant registers. They will often also try to *re-time* the resulting circuit: pushing combinatorial tasks before or after a delay register may help to balance signal delay paths and thus improve the maximum propagation delay, which is one of the key determinant for the circuit's speed.

Circuits generated this way typically serve as an entry point for further tuning. In particular, those circuits might have long and poorly balanced signal paths (despite automatic re-timing). And they do not leverage *parallelism*, which is a key strength of tailor-made hardware. In the section that follows, we will thus discuss how circuits can be optimized by exploiting *data parallelism* and *pipeline parallelism* (the latter also leads to optimized signal paths). But before that, we will have a very brief look at high-level synthesis tools.

4.2.3   HIGH-LEVEL SYNTHESIS

The aforementioned techniques are quite effective to build fast hardware circuits based on *data flow-oriented* task descriptions. By composing large circuits from smaller ones, even sizable application problems become manageable.

From a (software) programmer perspective, however, composition purely based on data flow is often counter-intuitive; an automated compiler that can handle control and data flow parts of a "conventional" programming language is clearly desirable. And indeed, several development platforms today offer *high-level language* compilers that can compile C, Java, or similar languages directly into a circuit description.

Much like a conventional software compiler, these systems usually turn the user program first into an internal representation consisting of *basic blocks* and annotated with *data flow* and *control flow* information. Figure 4.4 illustrates this for the Optimus compiler of Hormati et al. [2008]. The small code in Figure 4.4(a) results in four basic blocks as shown in Figure 4.4(b). The graph in Figure 4.4(b) is also annotated with control flow and data flow information (the latter only for variable *sum*).

To convert the sample code into a hardware circuit, Optimus will create a hardware unit for each block that adheres to a fixed port interface schema. This schema includes explicit ports for data and control flow information. Hardware units are finally wired up by connecting these ports according to the data and control flow information inferred from the user code. For more details refer to [Hormati et al., 2008].

High-level language synthesis becomes more effective if the starting language already contains mechanisms to, e.g., express independence of operations and/or parallelism. The Optimus compiler, for instance, is part of the *Liquid Metal* system of IBM Research [Auerbach et al., 2012] and comes with its own programming language *Lime* to express such properties. *Kiwi*, a

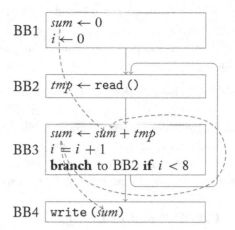

```
sum ← 0
for i = 0 to 7 do
    sum ← sum + read ()
end for
write (sum)
```

(a) Small example code with data and control flow.

(b) Basic blocks as inferred by Optimus, annotated with data flow information ⇠ ⇢ and control flow information ⟶.

Figure 4.4: To compile high-level language code, Optimus [Hormati et al., 2008] breaks down user code into *basic blocks* and annotates data flow and control flow information. After mapping all basic blocks to hardware, their control and data ports are wired according to the control and data flow information. Illustration adapted from [Hormati et al., 2008].

joint research project of U Cambridge and Microsoft Research [Greaves and Singh, 2008], uses custom attributes to .NET assembly to achieve the same goal.

The *Accelerator* platform[3] makes the interplay of language expressiveness and parallelism on different hardware back-ends explicit. In the context of .NET, *Accelerator* describes a functional-style framework to express data-parallel programs. A set of back-end compilers can then generate runnable code for a wide range of data-parallel hardware, including commodity processors, graphics processors, and FPGAs (the latter has been demonstrated by Singh [2011]).

4.3   DATA-PARALLEL APPROACHES

The strength of FPGAs (or any other bare-hardware platform) lies in their inherent hardware parallelism. Fundamentally, any single gate, any sub-circuit, or any sub-area on the chip die can operate independently of any other. This massive potential for parallelism is only limited by explicit synchronization or serialization, which the circuit designer chose to define to match the semantics of the application scenario.

In practice, application circuits do need a fair degree of synchronization. But hardware allows such synchronization to be lightweight and very efficient. This is in sharp contrast to heavyweight mechanisms (compare and swap or even just memory ordering), which program-

---

[3]http://research.microsoft.com/en-us/projects/Accelerator/

mers should avoid in software-based systems if they aim for performance. This capability for lightweight synchronization is also the reason why we are particularly interested in *fine-grained parallelism* in this chapter and look at task assignment on the level of assembly style micro-operations.

Types of Parallelism.   The available hardware parallelism can be applied to application problems in many different ways. In the context of FPGAs and tailor-made circuits, two strategies have been by far the most successful, and we will discuss them in turn. In this section, we first look at fine-grained *data parallelism*, which has many similarities to software techniques like vectorization or partition/replicate schemes. Section 4.4 then looks at *pipeline parallelism*, which in hardware is a lot more appealing than it typically is in software.

4.3.1   DATA PARALLELISM

There are many real-world situations where the *same* processing task has to be applied to all items in a data set. And with certain assumptions on independence and order indifference, hardware is free to handle individual items in parallel. The classical example to this are matrix or vector computations, where individual components can be calculated independently. Most tasks in the database domain can be handled this way, too; the relational data model, for instance, explicitly assumes set-oriented processing.

In the software domain, data parallelism has been successful at many levels. Vector processors operate on sets of data on the assembly level, a model that has been re-incarnated more recently in the form of SIMD capabilities for mainstream processors or in the form of data-parallel kernel execution on modern graphics processors (GPUs). Modern compilers allow us to parallelize situations of data parallelism across compute resources of multi-core architectures (an example tool kit is Intel's Thread Building Blocks library). And on the network scale, the MapReduce paradigm [Dean and Ghemawat, 2004] has written a remarkable story of success.

Data Parallelism in Hardware

On the hardware level, data parallelism corresponds to a *replication* of components on the chip area. This is illustrated in Figure 4.5 here on the right. Input data is distributed over the q replicas of the sub-circuit and processed in parallel. At the output, circuitry may be required to collect the results of parallel execution into a sequential output stream.

Replication allows us to linearly increase throughput by dedicating additional chip resources. q-fold replication roughly leads to a throughput improvement by a factor of

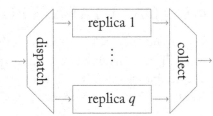

Figure 4.5: Circuit replication.

q (dispatch and collect logic can usually be integrated into surrounding components and thus be neglected).

Besides availability of chip space, the practical limit to replication is the speed at which data can be provided to the circuit and/or results consumed at the output of the circuit. For instance, if data arrive as a single, sequential input stream, dissecting this stream into independent work units often bottlenecks data-parallel execution.

4.4 PIPELINE-PARALLEL APPROACHES

Pipeline parallelism is a form of task parallelism and applies to situations where a given task f can be broken down into a sequence sub-tasks $f_1, \ldots, f_p$, such that $f = f_p \circ \cdots \circ f_1$. The sub-tasks $f_1, \ldots, f_p$ can then be computed on separate processing units, and intermediate results are forwarded from unit to unit (or pipeline stage to pipeline stage). The concept is similar to an assembly line in, say, a car factory. And like in a car factory, the concept becomes highly parallel if multiple data items flow through the pipeline one after another; all processing units then operate in parallel, each one on a different input item.

At the logical level, pipelining is a frequent pattern in many software systems. The execution engines of most database systems, for instance, are built on the concept and evaluate query plans in a pipeline model. Physically, however, those systems use pipelining only rarely. The cost of messaging between physical processing units is often prohibitive; forwarding database tuples, e.g., between processor cores would dominate the overall execution cost.

4.4.1 PIPELINE PARALLELISM IN HARDWARE

Between components of a hardware circuit, however, communication can be realized very efficiently, making pipeline parallelism a feasible concept even for very lightweight sub-tasks f_i. In fact, as we shall see in a moment, pipeline parallelism is the method of choice to gain performance in hardware circuits.

The reason for this is that pipeline parallelism becomes relatively easy to apply to a hardware circuit. To illustrate, suppose we are given a combinational circuit that performs an application task f. By re-grouping the gates and wirings into, say, three blocks, we can break up the computation of f into sub-circuits $f_1, \ldots, f_3$, even when their local semantics would be hard to express on the application level:

$$\rightarrow \boxed{f} \rightarrow \quad \rightsquigarrow \quad \rightarrow \boxed{f_1} \rightarrow \boxed{f_2} \rightarrow \boxed{f_3} \rightarrow \; .$$

To compute the f_i independent of one another (and thus allow for parallelism), as a next step we need to introduce *pipeline registers*. To this end, we insert a flip-flop on any signal path from f_i to f_{i+1}, as indicated here using gray bars:

$$\rightarrow \boxed{f_1} \;\vert\vert\; \boxed{f_2} \;\vert\vert\; \boxed{f_3} \rightarrow \; .$$

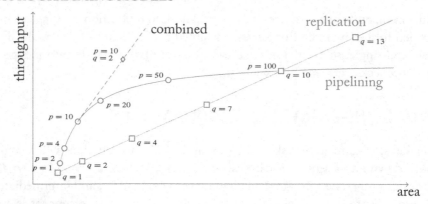

Figure 4.6: Effects of replication and pipelining on processing throughput of an example circuit. For this graph, we modeled an example circuit along the lines of Kaeslin [2008]. Notice that the location of, e.g., crossover points may depend on the particular circuit.

The effect of these registers is that they remember the outcome of computation f_i, such that in the following clock cycle they appear as a stable signal to the input of f_{i+1}. The circuit for f_i then becomes available again to accept the next item from its input.

Thus, the modified circuit could still accept a new input item on every clock cycle (like the original circuit f could). But the introduction of pipeline registers reduced the *longest signal path* of the circuit, which is now the longest path of any f_i. Assuming that f could be broken into subcircuits of equal size, this means that the *clock frequency* can be increased by approximately a factor of p (the pipeline depth). The increased clock frequency directly translates into a throughput increase.

Cost of Pipelining.   Pipelining is attractive in hardware, because the introduction of pipeline registers causes only a small overhead, both in terms of space and performance. Notice in particular that we only had to introduce new registers; there was no need to replicate or expand the combinational part of the circuit, however. Pipelining reaches its limit when the signal delay for a single f_i approaches the speed of the associated pipeline register.

This can be seen in Figure 4.6. In this figure, we illustrated how replication/data parallelism and pipelining can turn additional chip area into increased throughput. To obtain the graph, we assumed characteristics of a typical hardware circuit and idealized models for the effects of replication and pipelining, as detailed by Kaeslin [2008]. The graph shows how, initially, pipelining requires little investment (some flip-flops only) to gain substantial throughput improvements. The intrinsic latency of pipeline registers, however, limits the throughput that can be achieved with pipelining alone.

In practice, replication and pipelining are often used in combination. To illustrate, we included an example where the (pipelined) circuit with $p = 10$ is replicated on the chip, which for the example results in an additional performance boost.

Wiring Overhead.   The simple model used to generate Figure 4.6 does not include any overhead that may result from wiring and communication needs. If replication is used excessively, however, this overhead may become significant in practice, whereas pipeline parallelism tends to be less affected by wiring costs. This difference can be understood from the graphical representation that we showed above for both approaches. As the degree of parallelism increases replicated circuits will range over an increasing area of the chip die. Thus, dispatch and collect circuits at both ends have to bridge an increasing distance as q grows, which directly affects signal path lengths. This problem does not arise for pipeline parallelism, where communication remains short-ranged no matter how large the parallelism degree.

A practical example of how pipelining may actually help to avoid large fan-outs and long signal paths is the XML filtering engine that we showed earlier in Figure 4.3. Its actual implementation (detailed in [Teubner et al., 2012]) uses pipeline registers in-between segments of the state automaton circuit, as illustrated here on the right (Figure 4.7). The design avoids that the input stream must be supplied to all automaton transitions in parallel, which would scale poorly as the number of segments increases. This keeps throughput rates high, even when the length and complexity of the matching automaton increases [Teubner et al., 2012].

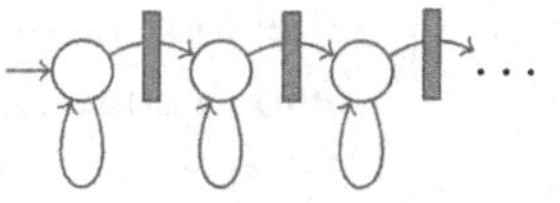

Figure   4.7: Pipelining and skeleton automata [Teubner et al., 2012].

4.4.2 PIPELINING IN FPGAS

The discussion above assumed that "chip space" can equally be used to instantiate (or replicate) logic or for additional flip-flops used as pipeline registers. In FPGAs, the amount and proportion of chip resources is fixed, however. Combinational logic resources cannot be re-purposed for flip-flops or vice versa.

In Section 3.3.1, we saw that actual FPGA devices are composed of *elementary logic units*, which refers to a static combination of lookup tables (i.e., combinational logic) and flip-flops that can latch the lookup table output. Enabling these flip-flops as pipeline registers, hence, will *not* increase the overall "chip space" demand of the circuit. At the same time, the size of an elementary logic unit lies within the sweet spot of pipelining, where combinational logic and register count are balanced to obtain a good area/throughput trade-off.

Good FPGA designs thus try to (quite aggressively) pipeline until the point where combinational logic and flip-flops are in balance. This explains, in other words, why the NFA construction mechanism of Yang and Prasanna [2012], which we looked at in Section 5.1.3, achieves favorable performance characteristics. The basic building blocks of this mechanism exactly match the lookup table/flip-flop combination within a typical elementary logic block. Observe how, in the same line of work, Yang et al. [2008] also bounded signal paths and fan-outs through pipelining (Figure 5.8).

4.4.3   DESIGNING FOR PIPELINE PARALLELISM

Pipeline parallelism is attractive also because—unlike data parallelism—it permits many forms of loop-carried dependencies. This is because, by construction, a data item that is processed at a pipeline stage f_i still "sees" any side effects that preceding items may have produced at f_i. To illustrate this with a toy example, the **for** clause in

> $sum \leftarrow 0$
> **for all** input items x **do**
> $\quad sum \leftarrow sum + x^2$
> **end for**

contains an inter-loop dependency (through variable sum) that violates the requirements for a data-parallel loop processing.

The loop body can, however, be broken down into two sub-operations that are evaluated in a pipeline fashion:

$$\longrightarrow \left(tmp \leftarrow x^2 \right) \longrightarrow \left(sum \leftarrow sum + tmp \right) \longrightarrow \ .$$

Pipeline registers in-between the two sub-operations would enable the loop body to be processed in parallel. In practice, operations like x^2 can be pipelined internally, increasing parallelism and speed even further.

Example: Pipeline-Parallel Frequent Item Computation

Arguably, the above example could be replaced by a parallel computation of partial sums, followed by a merging operation. The attractiveness of pipelining comes from the fact that also much more intricate application problems can be accelerated through pipeline parallelism. To illustrate this, consider the *Space-Saving* algorithm of Metwally et al. [2006], shown as Algorithm 1. To answer top-k-type queries, *Space-Saving* counts the number of occurrences of items x_i in a data stream. *Space-Saving* is an approximate algorithm with bounded space (n "bins," item/count pairs).

Space-Saving not only contains loop-carried dependencies (via count and item values). It also requires accessing the same memory content according to different criteria (item lookups and search for the bin with the minimum count value), which has made the algorithm notoriously hard to parallelize through classical means. In fact, the parallel solution of Das et al. [2009] has a lower throughput than the single-threaded code of Cormode and Hadjieleftheriou [2008], who did an in-depth study and comparison of frequent item counting techniques.

Pipeline parallelism can help to significantly speed up *Space-Saving* on FPGA hardware [Teubner et al., 2011]. The idea is a combination of classical pipeline parallelism—let input items x flow through a sequence of hardware-based bins—and a neighbor-to-neighbor communication mechanism between bins. The concept is illustrated in Figure 4.8. Items x_j travel along

for all input items x **do**
    find bin b_x with b_x.item $= x$
    if such a bin was found **then**
        b_x.count $\leftarrow b_x$.count $+ 1$
    else
        $b_{min} \leftarrow$ bin with minimum count value
        b_{min}.count $\leftarrow b_{min}$.count $+ 1$
        b_{min}.item $\leftarrow x$
    end if
end for

Algorithm 1: *Space-Saving* algorithm of Metwally et al. [2006].

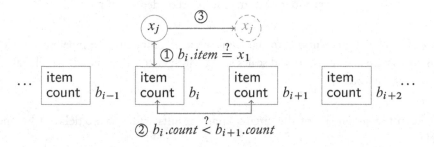

Figure 4.8: Pipeline-parallel implementation of *Space-Saving*. For each item x_j and bin b_i, ① compare x_j to the content of b_i, ② compare the count values of b_i and b_{i+1} (if necessary, swap bin contents so the smaller count value ends up on the right), then ③ forward x_j to b_{i+1}.

a pipeline of bins b_i. At every bin b_i, ① x_j is compared to the local item and the count value incremented if a match was found. Otherwise, ② the bin contents of b_i and b_{i+1} are compared according to their count values. If necessary, the contents of b_i and b_{i+1} are *swapped*, such that b_{i+1} receives the smaller count value. Then ③ the input item x_j moves on to the next bin b_{i+1}.

The frequent item example also nicely illustrates how pipeline parallelism can lead to significantly better scalability properties than data-parallel alternatives. In Teubner et al. [2011], we discussed various parallelization schemes for the problem on FPGA hardware. Figure 4.9 shows the scalability of the pipelined and data-parallel strategies of this comparative study.

4.4.4   TURNING A CIRCUIT INTO A PIPELINE-PARALLEL CIRCUIT

An electronic circuit reflects the *data flow* of the application problem that it implements. If this data flow is cycle-free, pipelining becomes straightforward and can be achieved as sketched at the beginning of Section 4.4.1. To this end, the circuit is "cut in half" in such a way that all signal wires which cross the cut have the same direction. A set of pipeline registers inserted into such

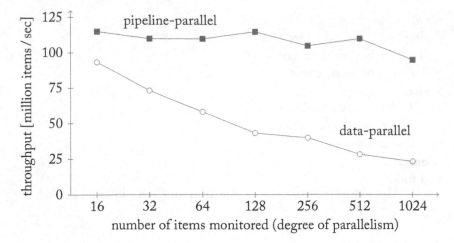

Figure 4.9: FPGA-based solutions to the frequent item problem. The pipeline-parallel strategy of Figure 4.8 keeps wire lengths short and scales significantly better than a data-parallel alternative (data from [Teubner et al., 2011]).

a cut will keep the semantics of the circuit intact; results will only be delayed by one additional clock cycle.

If the data flow contains cycles—that is, if the output of a previous computation is needed to process the next input item—such cuts may no longer be found, and the intuitive approach to pipelining no longer be successful. It turns out, however, that many forms of such *recursive* circuits can still be pipelined. A good starting point to get to a pipelined solution is to partially unroll the iterative computation. Depending on additional properties, such as associativity of operations, the unrolled circuit can then often be re-organized such that "cuts" in the above sense can be found. A detailed discussion is beyond the scope of this book and we refer to Section 2.7 in the book of Kaeslin [2008] for details.

4.5   RELATED CONCEPTS

In many ways, FPGAs are probably the most flexible type of compute resources available today. As such, they cover a very large design space in terms of their system design and integration and in terms of how they exploit hardware parallelism, which has become the key approach to performance in virtually any computing device.

Several specific points in this design space are also covered by off-the-shelf hardware devices that may be usable as accelerators, co-processors, or even standalone processors. Probably the most well-known representatives of such a device are *graphics processors (GPUs)*, which meanwhile have evolved into computing platforms with a remarkably wide range of applications.

Graphics Processors (GPUs).   Graphics processing units make *data parallelism* explicit at a scale unmatched by any other processor technology. The latest incarnation of the NVIDIA Kepler architecture, for instance, includes up to 15 "SMX Streaming Multiprocessors" [Corp., 2012]. Each of them contains 192 "cores" (which in general-purpose CPU terminology would best compare to an ALU), for a total of 2,880 parallel processing units. Thereby, the granularity of data parallelism sits in-between the replicated parallel circuits that we discussed in Section 4.3 and the course-grained parallelism available in general-purpose multi-core processors. NVIDIA GPUs follow an SIMT ("single instruction, multiple threads") execution model: groups of 32 threads (a "warp") are scheduled such that *all* 32 threads execute the *same* instruction at the same time. This significantly eases hardware scheduling logic and brings intrinsic data parallelism all the way down to the execution layer.

At the programmer's level, the graphics device can execute *compute kernels*. Many thousands, even millions or more, logical executions of such a kernel operate on independent data items. Thereby, synchronization across threads is highly limited, which again simplifies the underlying hardware and enables higher compute density.

Graphics processors were identified as a potential substrate for database co-processing almost a decade ago. Govindaraju et al. [2004] showed—even before graphics processors offered the programmability that they have today—that the available data parallelism can be used to speed up important database tasks, such as selection and aggregation. Two years later, Govindaraju et al. [2006] showed how the use of a GPU co-processor can offer significant performance/price advantages when implementing *sorting*. He et al. [2008] pushed the idea of using graphics processors for database co-processing one step further by running *database joins* on GPU hardware.

Many-Core Processors.   Inspired by graphics processor designs, other processor makers have come up with acceleration platforms that emphasize data parallelism on the hardware level. Intel has recently announced their *Xeon Phi* platform [Intel Corp., 2012], which packages 60 general-purpose cores, each capable of executing four threads, into a single chip. Internally, each core offers a 512-bit-wide SIMD unit for vector-oriented execution. While the processing model of Xeon Phi is not strictly tied to data-parallel execution, its NUMA (non-uniform memory access) architecture clearly favors data-parallel tasks.

Data Flow Computing on FPGAs.   For reasons mentioned in this chapter, FPGAs are very attractive to leverage pipeline parallelism (and accelerate application tasks that can benefit less from data parallelism alone). Several vendors make this explicit in FPGA programming platforms. For instance, Maxeler offers platforms for *dataflow computing* [Pell and Averbukh, 2012]. A dedicated compiler extracts data flow information from a Java program. The resulting data flow graph is then mapped to an FPGA circuit design that is highly susceptible to pipeline parallelism. Processing pipelines created this way may span entire FPGA chip dies and use thousands of pipeline stages.

CHAPTER 5

Data Stream Processing

FPGA technology can be leveraged in modern computing systems by using them as a *co-processor* (or "accelerator") in a heterogeneous computing architecture, where CPUs, FPGAs, and possibly further hardware components are used jointly to solve application problems.

This idea is particularly attractive for application settings that readily match the strengths of programmable hardware. This has led the research community to specifically investigate into *streaming scenarios*, where data arrives as a continuous flow and has to be processed in real time. Flow-oriented processing can leverage the *I/O capabilities* of modern FPGA devices, and if the necessary amount of *state* can be kept (mostly) within the device, an FPGA-based stream processor will not suffer from *von Neumann* or *memory bottlenecks*.

In this chapter, we look at some systems that have applied this idea successfully to important application problems. We start by showing how FPGAs can accelerate pattern matching in *network intrusion detection* systems (Section 5.1), then lift the ideas to support *complex event processing*, which lies at the heart of many stream processing engines (Section 5.2). In Sections 5.3 through 5.5, we will generalize the use of FPGAs for data flow problems and illustrate how *SQL-style query functionality* can be realized with the help of FPGAs.

5.1   REGULAR EXPRESSION MATCHING

Matching an input data stream to a (set of) *regular expression(s)* is an important and useful task on its own, but also as a pre-processing step for many stream analysis tasks. For instance, it is the task of a *network intrusion detection* system to detect suspicious patterns in a network data flow and perform a series of actions when a match is detected (e.g., alert users or block network traffic). Semantically rich stream processing engines depend on parsing and value extraction from their input stream to perform higher-level computations.

Regular expressions correspond 1-to-1 to *finite-state automata*, which are the method of choice to realize pattern matching in both hard- and software. Their low-level implementation faces considerably different trade-offs in hard- and software. By studying these trade-offs, in the following we illustrate some of the important characteristics of FPGA hardware and their consequences on real-world applications.

5.1.1   FINITE-STATE AUTOMATA FOR PATTERN MATCHING

Figure 5.1 illustrates how finite-state automata and regular expressions relate. The automaton shown implements the regular expression .*abac.*d. It is an instance of a *non-deterministic*

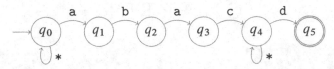

Figure 5.1: Non-deterministic automaton, corresponding to the regular expression `.*abac.*d`.

finite-state automaton (NFA). That is, multiple states in this automaton might be active at a time (e.g., after reading a single a, states q_0 and q_1 are both active) and multiple transitions may have to be followed for a single input symbol.

A beauty of non-deterministic automata lies in their easy derivation from regular expressions. Simple, syntax-driven construction rules—most well known are those of McNaughton and Yamada [1960] and Thompson [1968]—allow to mechanically convert any regular pattern into an equivalent NFA. This simplicity is the reason why in Figure 5.1, the original pattern `.*abac.*d` still shines through. For similar reasons, such non-deterministic automata are attractive in many application scenarios, because new patterns can easily be added (or old ones removed) from an existing automaton.

Deterministic and Non-Deterministic Automata

On the flip side, non-deterministic automata are less straightforward to implement in computer software. To process an input symbol, all candidate states and transitions have to be considered iteratively by a software program. This is inefficient by itself and will likely break the $\mathcal{O}(1)$ cost characteristics (per input symbol) promised by regular expressions and state automata.

Most software systems resolve this inefficiency by converting the generated NFA into a *deterministic finite-state automaton (DFA)*. In a DFA, exactly one state is active at any time, and exactly one transition has to be followed for every input symbol. Systems can exploit this property and implement input processing as a series of lookups in a ⟨*old-state, symbol*⟩ → *new-state* mapping table (e.g., realized through a hash table). An NFA can be converted into a DFA, e.g., by powerset construction: given an NFA with states $q_i^N \in S^N$, each subset of (active) states corresponds to exactly one element in the powerset $Q^D := 2^{Q^N}$.[1]

Figure 5.2 illustrates the result of such a conversion (we simplified the automaton by eliminating unreachable DFA states). The illustration shows that the conversion increases the number of automaton states. Further, the correspondence to the original pattern has largely gone lost in the conversion process.

---

[1]In practice, many states in Q^D can be determined statically to be unreachable, so the actual number of states $|Q^D|$ is typically less than $2^{|Q^N|}$.

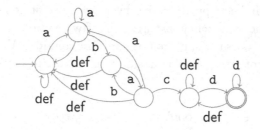

Figure 5.2: Deterministic automaton, equivalent to the non-deterministic automaton in Figure 5.1. The automaton contains more states, but now only one of them can be active at a time.

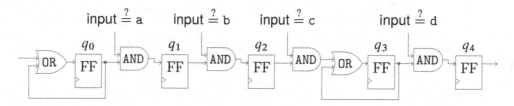

Figure 5.3: Hardware implementation for the non-deterministic automaton in Figure 5.1. Each state q_i maps to a flip-flop register; each transition maps to combinational logic between states.

5.1.2   IMPLEMENTING FINITE-STATE AUTOMATA IN HARDWARE

FPGAs can be viewed as essentially a generic implementation of a finite-state automaton in hardware. In fact, *any* logic circuit strictly is not more than a finite-state automaton (since the available amount of memory is finite). As such, it is only natural to implement user-level automata using configurable logic.

A given automaton can be mapped to an equivalent hardware circuit mechanically in the following way (this construction assumes that ε transitions have been eliminated beforehand, as it is the case in Figure 5.1):

1. For each automaton state q_i, instantiate a *flip-flop register* FF_i. Each flip-flop can hold one bit of information, which we interpret as *active/inactive*.

2. For each transition $q_i \xrightarrow{p} q_j$, instantiate combinational logic that forwards an *active* bit from FF_i to FF_j if the condition p is satisfied. If the new content of FF_j has multiple sources, combine them with a logical OR.

Applying this strategy to the automaton in Figure 5.1 results in the hardware logic shown in Figure 5.3. Observe how the construction preserves the structure of the source automaton and how states/transitions map to flip-flops/combinational logic.

An automaton can be mapped into hardware with this strategy whether the automaton is deterministic or not. The inefficiency that arises in software implementations—iterative processing of candidate states—does not apply to this hardware solution. All logic resources in an FPGA chip operate independently, so possible transitions are naturally considered in parallel.

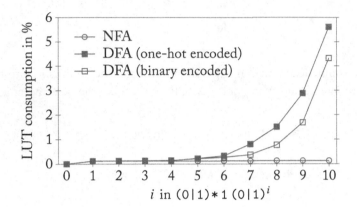

Figure 5.4: FPGA resource consumption (lookup tables) for automaton alternatives. DFAs can be encoded with one bit per state (one-hot) or by enumerating all states and encoding them in a binary number.

In fact, when implemented in hardware, non-deterministic automata are often the strategy of choice. In addition to the advantages already mentioned above (correspondence with regular expressions allows for easy construction or modification), NFAs tend to have a much simpler structure. This makes the combinational logic to implement transitions simpler and more efficient.[2] In Figure 5.4, we illustrated the FPGA resource demand for different implementation strategies for the same regular expression (Xilinx Virtex-5 LX110T chip). Consumption of logic resources is an important criterion in FPGA design on its own. Here the growing logic complexity may additionally lead to longer signal propagation delays, reduced clock frequencies, and lower overall performance.

5.1.3 OPTIMIZED CIRCUIT CONSTRUCTION

Early on, alternative construction mechanisms were suggested that allow us to turn a given regular expression into a hardware implementation directly, without explicitly building an automaton as we saw in Figure 5.1. Such a direct construction is particularly meaningful for programmable logic, such as programmable logic arrays (PLAs; addressed by Floyd and Ullman [1982]) or FPGAs (which are the target of the technique of Sidhu and Prasanna [2001]).

---

[2]Note that the number of states does not directly make a difference. An NFA with $|Q^N|$ states may lead to a DFA with $2^{|Q^N|}$ states. But since only one of them can be active at any time, $|Q^N|$ bits still suffice to encode the current state.

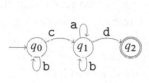

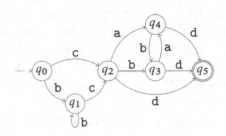

(a) Simplified NFA to match the regular expression b*c(a|b)*d.

(b) NFA for b*c(a|b)*d where all transitions incoming to one state carry the same condition.

Figure 5.5: Rewriting finite-state automata for better FPGA resource utilization. Both automata recognize the same language, but the right one maps better to FPGA primitives.

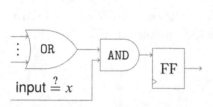

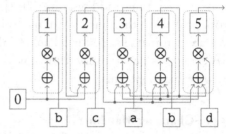

(a) Hardware module to implement NFA.

(b) Automaton for expression b*c(a|b)*d, built from modules shown on the left.

Figure 5.6: Once NFAs are in proper shape (cf. Figure 5.5(b)), they can be realized just with the single type of module shown as (a). Figure (b) illustrates the resulting implementation of b*c(a|b)*d (where ⊕ abbreviates an OR gate and ⊗ stands for an AND gate).

The utilization of FPGA logic resources can be improved if the construction is designed to match the basic FPGA primitives. In particular, combinational logic is available in FPGAs in the form of n-input lookup tables, which are typically paired with a flip-flop register (in Xilinx FPGAs, this makes the basic building block of an FPGA *slice*). A method to do so was suggested by Yang and Prasanna [2012], Yang et al. [2008]. They observed that the NFA for any user pattern can be brought into a particular shape, namely such that for each state, all of its input transitions have to match the same input symbol.

Formally, in a finite-state automaton, each input symbol x_i brings the automaton from one state q_i to another, q_{i+1}. The new state is defined by a transition function f:

$$q_{i+1} = f(q_i, x_i) \ . \tag{5.1}$$

Figure 5.5 illustrates this with two automata for the regular expression b*c(a|b)*d. Intuitively, the automaton in Figure 5.5(a) has lower resource consumption. But the alternative in

Figure 5.5(b) satisfies the constraint of having just one input symbol at the incoming transitions of each automaton state. Automata that adhere to this shape can be realized in hardware with just a single type of module. Such a module is shown in Figure 5.6(a) (assuming an n-ary OR gate to accommodate ingoing transitions and an AND gate to account for the condition). As Yang and Prasanna [2012] have shown, the combinational parts of this circuit map well to a combination of lookup tables, which are readily paired with a flip-flop in modern FPGAs. Figure 5.6(b) shows how modules can be assembled to implement the automaton shown in Figure 5.5(b).

5.1.4   NETWORK INTRUSION DETECTION

Regular expression matching forms the heart of most *publish/subscribe systems*, where "subscribers" register patterns that describe which parts of a stream they are interested in. A particular use case is *network intrusion detection*, where the set of subscriptions is a rule set that describes known network attacks. Yang and Prasanna [2012], Yang et al. [2008] have shown how the matching of network packets to this rule set can be realized in FPGA hardware. Beyond design internals of finite-state automata (as discussed above), these implementations also give a good sense of how FPGA circuits can be optimized and how design trade-offs are considerably different from those in software-based systems.

Multiple-Character Matching

Following Equation 5.1, state q_{i+2} can be obtained by applying f twice,

$$q_{i+1} = f(q_{i+1}, x_{i+1}) = f\big(f(q_i, x_i), x_{i+1}\big) \stackrel{\text{def}}{=} F(q_i, x_i, x_{i+1}) \, ,$$
$$(5.2)$$

and consuming *two* input symbols at once.

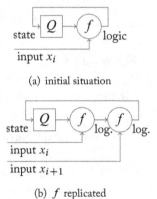

(a) initial situation

(b) f replicated

Figure 5.7: Two input symbols per clock cycle.

If realized in software, F might be difficult to construct and require a very large lookup table. In hardware, by contrast, the concept is rather simple to implement. Figure 5.7(a) shows a high-level view of a hardware state automaton, grouping the circuit into *state* (flip-flop registers Q) and combinational *logic* that implements the transition function f. As can be seen in the figure, f consumes the initial state and an input symbol x_i to compute a new state (as in Equation 5.1).

The situation in Equation 5.2 can now be obtained by *replicating* the logic associated with f. As shown in Figure 5.7(b), this means that the resulting hardware circuit can now consume two input symbols in a single clock cycle. In practice, this trades higher chip space consumption for better matching throughput.

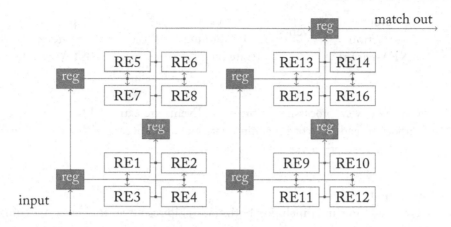

Figure 5.8: Pipeline registers (indicated as) help to keep signal propagation delays low and avoid high-fanout signals (illustration adapted from Yang et al. [2008]).

Signal Propagation Delays and Pipelining

Actual intrusion detection systems will have to match the input network stream against hundreds, if not thousands, of rules. With the amount of chip space available in modern FPGAs, all state automata to match such large rule sets can be laid out side-by-side on the two-dimensional chip area. Thanks to the intrinsic parallelism, all rules can then be matched fully in parallel, promising high, rule set-independent matching speed.

In practice, however, such perfect scaling is limited by geometrical and physical effects. As the rule set grows, the generated automata will cover a growing area on the chip, causing the *distance* between components to increase (following an $\mathcal{O}(N)$ dependence, where N is the number of NFAs). This, in turn, increases *signal propagation delays* in the generated circuit, such that the *clock frequency* (and thus the achievable throughput) has to be reduced to maintain correct behavior of the hardware circuit.

A solution to this problem is *pipelining*. Thereby, signal paths are intercepted by *pipeline registers*, which memorize their input signals from one clock cycle to the next. With shorter signal paths, clock frequencies can be increased, with direct consequences on the observed throughput. The price for this is a slight increase in latency. In an *n*-staged pipeline, the overall circuit output (in this case a match information) is delayed by *n* FPGA clock cycles.

For the problem at hand, pipelining can be applied in a hierarchical fashion, as illustrated in Figure 5.8. As can be seen in the figure, this keeps the number of stages (intuitively, the number of pipeline registers along any path from the circuit input to its output) short, while still allowing for a large rule set. In practice, clock cycle times are in the range 5–10 ns, such that pipelining causes only negligible latency overhead (e.g., compared to the time the same packet needs to travel over the network wire).

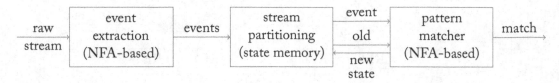

Figure 5.9: Complex event processing architecture. Events are extracted from raw input stream. A partitioner component reads the corresponding state for each input event, hands it to an NFA-based pattern matcher, then memorizes the new partition state.

Space ↔ Throughput

Multi-character matching and pipelining both trade chip resources for better matching through-put. As a third space ↔ throughput trade-off, the entire matching logic can be replicated on the chip, with incoming network packets load-balanced to either of the replicas. In practice, all three strategies form a design space, and it depends on the hardware and problem characteristic, which combination of strategies maximizes the overall matching throughput. For a rule set of 760 patterns from the SNORT intrusion detection system, Yang et al. [2008] report an achievable throughput of 14.4 Gb/s on a Virtex-4 LX100 FPGA device (this chip was released in 2004).

5.2 COMPLEX EVENT PROCESSING

As described above, finite-state automata allow the detection of symbol sequences in a single input data stream. This model is adequate, e.g., to perform syntactic analyses on the stream or to match patterns within a single message (as is the case in the above intrusion detection scenario). The true strength of modern stream processing engines, however, comes from lifting pattern matching to a higher semantical level. To this end, low-level *events* are derived from the input stream (e.g., through syntactic analyses). The resulting sequence of events is then analyzed according to *complex event patterns*. As an example, a stock broker might want to be informed whenever the price for any stock symbol has seen five or more upward movements, then a downward change (pattern up{5} down, where up and down are derived events).

The challenge in matching complex event patterns is that they usually depend on semantic *partitioning* of the input events. For instance, prices for various stock symbols might arrive interleaved with one another; a matching pattern for one stock symbol might overlap with many (partial) matches for other symbols. To detect such patterns, the stream processor needs to keep track of the matching state for each of the stock symbols in the stream.

5.2.1 STREAM PARTITIONING

To realize semantic stream partitioning, Woods et al. [2010] devised a *partitioner* component that plugs into the data flow of the stream processing system.

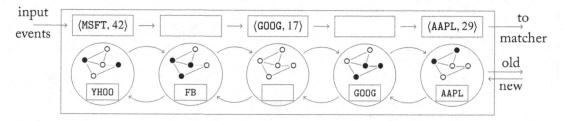

Figure 5.10: Hardware-based stream partitioning using a chain of ⟨*group-id, state-vec*⟩ pairs. The strategy keeps signal paths short and the design scalable.

The resulting architecture is illustrated in Figure 5.9. An NFA-based syntax analyzer extracts low-level events from the raw input stream (e.g., a network byte stream, as used for click stream analysis in [Woods et al., 2011]). A hardware stream partitioner uses the partitioning criterion in each event (e.g., a stock symbol or a client IP address) to read out the current vector of states from a local state memory. State vector and source event are then routed to the actual pattern matcher which will *(a)* report eventual matches to the outside and *(b)* send an updated state vector back to the partitioner component.

5.2.2 HARDWARE PARTITIONER

To sustain real-world input data rates, such as the line rate of a monitored network port, state lookups and write-backs must adhere to tight performance constraints. On the one hand, this rules out typical approaches that are optimized for average-case performance in software solutions, such as hash tables. On the other hand, the intrinsic parallelism of FPGA hardware allows us to perform a large number of (lookup) tasks in parallel. Woods et al. [2010] showed how this FPGA feature can be used to guarantee line-rate processing for hundreds of stream partitions, with the only limit being the available chip space.

The idea of this approach is illustrated in Figure 5.10. ⟨*group-id, state-vec*⟩ pairs are organized as a chain of hardware components. Incoming events (containing a group id and further semantic content) are handed from one element in this chain to the next, one every FPGA clock cycle. The key idea is that chain elements can be *swapped* under certain conditions. Swapping means that two neighboring elements exchange their contents (state vector and group id).

In our case, whenever a *group-id* matches the one in the passing-by event, we swap that element toward the end of the chain. Thus, when the event has been propagated through the entire chain, the last element will contain its associated state vector. From there, both event and state vector are handed over to the NFA that performs the actual pattern matching.

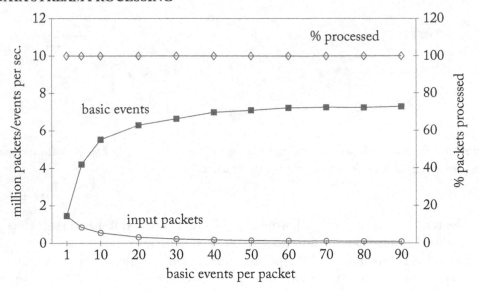

Figure 5.11: Complex event processing in hardware guarantees line-rate performance, independent of how events are packeted on the network wire. Results taken from Woods et al. [2011].

5.2.3 BEST-EFFORT ALLOCATION

The chain of ⟨*group-id, state-vec*⟩ pairs defines a fixed number of partitions (e.g., the number of distinct stock symbols) that can be monitored concurrently. These available chain elements are allocated dynamically based on incoming events. To this end, elements are not only swapped when they match the group id of a passing-by event, but also when they have not yet been assigned to any group id. In Figure 5.10, for instance, the event ⟨GOOG, 17⟩ may have pushed the still-empty element in the middle to its current position. As a consequence, when an event reaches the right end of the chain, it will find there either its matching state vector or a vacant chain element, which will then be allocated for the respective group id.

Some input streams may exceed the hardware limit on the number of group ids (many hundreds, in practice). In such cases, chain elements can be allocated using a *best-effort strategy*, where recently seen group ids are prioritized over very old ones. Such best-effort allocation can be achieved with a simple timeout counter associated with each chain element [Woods et al., 2010].

5.2.4 LINE-RATE PERFORMANCE

A key selling point of hardware-based solutions are their strong performance guarantees, even under unforeseen load characteristics. In the case of monitoring or event processing applications, the ability to process input data at full line rate is particularly desirable.

The hardware partitioning mechanism illustrated above was shown to guarantee such line-rate performance, as illustrated in Figure 5.11. Software-based alternatives are often very sensitive to the way events are presented at the input of the system. If events are sent as very small Ethernet packets, for instance, most software solutions become overloaded because of their high per-packet processing overhead. As the figure shows, hardware-accelerated complex event processing is not sensitive to this problem and guarantees 100 % line rate performance independent of event packeting.

5.3   FILTERING IN THE DATA PATH

Up until now we had looked at the FPGA as an isolated component. It would listen to an incoming stream, but we left unspecified what kind of "output" or "action" is being generated by the programmable hardware. In practice, most applications will be too complex to be solved entirely in FPGA hardware, which suggests *hybrid FPGA/CPU processing* to jointly solve the application task. Ideally, a hybrid system design would also allow for a *transition path*, where performance-critical functionality is off-loaded one-by-one without major disruptions on the user-level interface.

A system architecture that can satisfy all these criteria is when the FPGA is plugged into the *data path* of the processing engine:

In such an architecture, the FPGA consumes the raw input data—usually high-volume—and applies filtering or other pre-processing steps that reduce the volume of data. The remaining low-volume data set is forwarded to a conventional CPU, where, for instance, it could be fed into the processing pipeline of an existing system. A practical example of this model could be an FPGA that applies selection and projection to a large data set while it is read from a hard disk (i.e., source ≡ disk). Netezza commercialized this concept in their *Netezza Performance Server (NPS)* system.

A data path architecture elegantly separates the application task to match the strengths of both parts of an FPGA/CPU hybrid. FPGAs are extremely good when the task to perform is relatively simple, but the data volume is huge. Conversely, sophisticated control logic in general-purpose processors makes them very efficient at complex operations; but their I/O capabilities and their energy efficiency fall way behind those of modern FPGA devices.

5.3.1   DATA PATH ARCHITECTURE IN THE REAL WORLD

Architecting an FPGA/CPU hybrid along its data path fits well also with "needle in a haystack" application patterns that are becoming dominant in many business domains. Event processing systems need to sift through large amounts of dynamic data, but typically only few events are actually relevant for further processing. High expectations toward ad hoc querying force data analytics engines to execute most of their work as brute force scans over large data volumes (Unterbrunner et al. [2009] describe a flight booking system as a concrete example).

Electronic stock trading is a prototype example of how FPGAs can significantly accelerate existing application systems or even enable new market opportunities that will remain hard to address with software-only solutions even in upcoming CPU architectures. The challenge here is a very high input data volume, combined with uniquely tight latency requirements. Any improvement in latency—on a micro-second scale!—will bring a competitive advantage that may be worth millions of dollars [Schneider, 2012].

High-Frequency Trading.   In *high-frequency trading*, stock traders monitor market price information. Automated systems buy or sell stocks within fractions of a milli-second to, e.g., benefit from arbitrage effects. These systems usually focus on a very particular market segment, stock symbol, or class of shares. If the input stream from the stock market—typically a high-volume stream with information about a large market subset—is pre-processed on an FPGA and with negligible latency, the core trading system can focus just on the relevant parts of the market, with lower latency and better forecasting precision.

Risk Management.   In response to incidents on the stock market, where erroneous trades by automated systems have led to severe market disruptions (e.g., the May 6, 2010 "Flash Crash" or a technology breakdown at Knight Capital Group on August 1, 2012), the American SEC began to impose *risk management* controls on stock brokers. Today, any broker with direct market access has to sanity-check all orders sent to the stock market to prevent unintended large-scale stock orders (SEC Rule 15c3-5).

Software alone would not be able to evaluate all SEC criteria without adding significant latency to the trading process. But if the control program "listens in" to the trading stream through an FPGA with pre-processing capabilities, risk evaluation can be performed with a latency of only a micro-second or less [Lockwood et al., 2012].

5.4   DATA STREAM PROCESSING

For certain application areas—we discussed network monitoring and electronic stock trading here—FPGAs offer significant advantages in terms of performance, but also in terms of their energy efficiency. Ideally, these advantages would carry over to more general cases of stream or database processing.

This is exactly the goal of the *Glacier* system [Mueller et al., 2009, 2010]. *Glacier* is a compiler that can translate queries from a dialect of SQL into the VHDL description of an equivalent hardware circuit. This circuit, when loaded into an FPGA, implements the given query in hardware and at a guaranteed throughput rate.

Table 5.1: Streaming algebra supported by the *Glacier* SQL-to-hardware compiler (a, b, c: field names; q, q_i: sub-plans; x: parameterized sub-plan input). Taken from [Mueller et al., 2009].

operator	semantics
$\pi_{a_1,...,a_n}(q)$	projection
$\sigma_a(q)$	select tuples where field a contains true
$\bigstar_{a:(b_1,b_2)}(q)$	arithmetic/Boolean operation $a = b_1 \star b_2$
$q_1 \cup q_2$	union
$agg_{b:a}(q)$	aggregate *agg* using input field a, $agg \in \{\texttt{avg}, \texttt{count}, \texttt{max}, \texttt{min}, \texttt{sum}\}$
$q_1 \text{ grp}_{x\mid c} q_2(x)$	group output of q_1 by field c, then invoke q_2 with x substituted by the group
$q_1 \boxplus^t_{x\mid k,l} q_2(x)$	sliding window with size k, advance by l; apply q_2 with x substituted on each window; $t \in \{\text{time}, \text{tuple}\}$: time- or tuple-based
$q_1 \otimes q_2$	concatenation; position-based field join

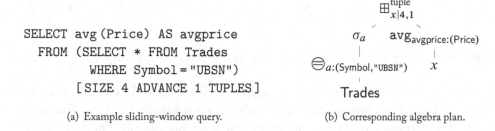

```
SELECT avg(Price) AS avgprice
  FROM (SELECT * FROM Trades
        WHERE Symbol = "UBSN")
        [SIZE 4 ADVANCE 1 TUPLES]
```

(a) Example sliding-window query.

(b) Corresponding algebra plan.

Figure 5.12: Query compilation in *Glacier*. Streaming SQL queries are converted into an algebraic representation, then compiled into a hardware circuit.

The heart of the *Glacier* compiler operates on a streaming algebra that assumes tuple-structured input events. This algebra, shown in Table 5.1, is sufficient to express particularly those aspects of a user query that can be realized as a pre-processing step in the sense of the data path architecture discussed above. Operators can be nested arbitrarily. Following the usual design of a database-style query processor, SQL queries stated by the user are first converted into an internal algebraic form, then translated to VHDL code. Figure 5.12 illustrates an example adapted from Mueller et al. [2009] and its corresponding algebraic plan.

5.4.1   COMPOSITIONAL QUERY COMPILATION

Glacier derives its power from the ability to translate the aforementioned algebra in a fully compositional manner. To this end, the hardware equivalent for every compiled algebra (sub-)expression follows the same *wiring interface*, which is sketched in Figure 5.13. Each *n*-bit-wide tuple is represented as a set of *n* parallel wires on the hardware side. An additional data_valid line signals the presence of a tuple in the remaining wires. For every algebraic operator ⊗, *Glacier* knows a set of compilation rules that produces the wiring interface in Figure 5.13, provided that the operands of ⊗ are already compiled according to that interface.

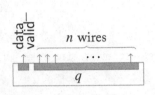

Figure 5.13: Wiring interface in *Glacier*.

Figure 5.14 illustrates two such compilation rules. The rule on the left (translating the selection operator σ) uses an AND gate to set the data_valid line to false if the selection condition is not met, thus invalidating the respective tuple.[3] The projection operator π effectively drops columns from the relation schema. In hardware, this can be achieved by simply not wiring up the respective signals to any upstream operator, as shown in the right rule in Figure 5.14.

Figure 5.14: *Glacier* compilation rules for *selection* (left) and *projection* (right).

This compilation rule for algebraic projection illustrates an interesting interplay between query compilation into a logical hardware circuit and the subsequent compilation stages (synthesis, map, and place & route) that generate the actual physical circuit. For many reasons, "loose wires" often occur in generated hardware circuits. FPGA design tools thus optimize out all subcircuits whose output is not connected to any outside port. *Glacier*'s compilation rule for projection takes advantage of this feature. Effectively, *Glacier* off-loads *projection pushdown*—a well-known database optimization strategy—to the FPGA design tools.

Push-Based Execution Strategy

Glacier-generated hardware execution plans follow a strictly *push-based* execution strategy. That is, individual sub-plans write their output into a single register set, from where they assume an upstream operator will pick up the result immediately in the next clock cycle.

Such a strategy is adequate for execution in hardware, because a circuit's runtime characteristics can be inferred statically at circuit generation time with very high accuracy. More specif-

---

[3]Note that in the *Glacier* algebra, σ operates on Boolean columns only. Complex selection criteria must be made explicit by applying, e.g., arithmetic or Boolean operations beforehand.

ically, the *latency*, i.e., the number of clock cycles needed by an operator to present the result of a computation at its output port, and the *issue rate*, i.e., the minimum gap (in clock cycles) between two successive tuples pushed into an operator, are precisely defined by the structure of the hardware circuit. *Glacier* submits the generated hardware description together with the desired *clock frequency* (e.g., sufficient to meet the line rate of a network data stream) to the FPGA tool chain, which will verify that the generated circuit can meet the frequency requirements. If a circuit cannot meet its requested throughput rate, the situation will be detected at compile time and the user demand rejected by the *Glacier* system.

For most query types, *Glacier* can maintain an issue rate of one tuple per clock cycle [Mueller et al., 2009] (which in practice significantly eases timing and interfacing with the respective stream source). Typical queries roughly compile into a pipeline-style query plan, which means that the latency of the generated plan depends linearly on the query complexity. In practice, the resulting latencies are rarely a concern; for clock frequencies of 100–200 MHz, a few cycles (typically less than a hundred) still result in a latency of less than a micro-second.

Resource Management

Glacier draws its predictable runtime performance from statically allocating *all* hardware resources at circuit compilation time. Each operator instance, for example, receives its dedicated chip area and no resources are shared between operators.[4] In effect, the compiler lays out a hardware plan on the two-dimensional chip space with a structure that resembles the shape of the input algebra plan. Processed data flows through this plan, resulting in a truly pipelined query execution.

Resource management becomes an issue mainly in the context of stateful operators such as *grouping* (aggregation) or *windowing*. *Glacier* assumes that the necessary state for such operations can be determined at query compilation time (e.g., with knowledge about group cardinalities or from the combination of window and slide sizes in the case of windowing operators). *Glacier* then *replicates* dependent sub-plans and produces a *dispatch* logic that routes tuples to any involved replica.

Figure 5.15 illustrates this mechanism for the query shown earlier in Figure 5.12. The bottom part of this generated hardware execution plan reflects the σ-$\ominus$ combination (this part will result in strictly pipelined processing). The upper part contains five replicas of the avg sub-plan (the windowing clause 4, 1 allows at most four windows to be open at any time) and dispatch logic to drive them. For windowing operators, the dispatch logic consists of *cyclic shift registers (CSRs)* that let windows open and close according to the windowing clause given.

In the case of *windowing* clauses, *Glacier* will route tuples to sub-circuits for all active windows and typically many of them are active at a time. For *grouping* operations, by contrast, tuples must be routed to exactly one group. *Glacier* still uses circuit replication to represent grouping in hardware (and a content-addressable memory (CAM) to look up matching groups). If replica-

---

[4]*Glacier* does allow a restricted form of multi-query optimization. Because of the strictly push-based processing model, identical sub-plans can be shared across queries.

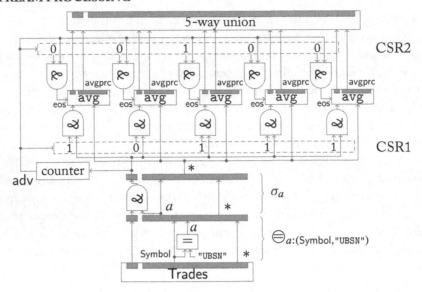

Figure 5.15: Hardware execution plan for the query in Figure 5.12(a). *Glacier* replicates the sub-plan of the windowing operator ⊞. A combination of two *cyclic shift registers (CSR)* routes tuples to the right replica(s). Illustration adapted from [Mueller et al., 2009].

tion is not desirable (or not feasible, e.g., because of hardware resource constraints), the hardware partitioning mechanism discussed in Section 5.2.2 could be used to memorize group states and create only one circuit instance to serve all groups.

Hash Tables in Hardware.   For even larger groups, circuits may have to resort to external memory to keep group states. A *hash table* would be the obvious choice for a data structure for this purpose. The crux of hashing is, however, its unpredictable performance. Hash collisions may require multiple round trips to memory, leading to a response time dependence on key distributions.

Kirsch and Mitzenmacher [2010] describe and analyze hashing schemes for hardware implementations. If used correctly, *multiple-choice hashing schemes* can significantly reduce the probability of hash collisions. And once collisions have become very rare (Kirsch and Mitzenmacher [2010] report probabilities below one in a million entries), a small content-addressable memory (CAM), installed side-by-side to the hash table, is enough to capture them. This way, predictable performance can be achieved with minimal hardware resource consumption.

In multiple-choice hashing schemes, every key has multiple locations where it could be placed in memory. Cuckoo hashing [Pagh and Rodler, 2001] is a known software technique based on multiple-choice hashing to guarantee constant-time lookups. When realized in hardware, all possible locations of an entry can be tested in parallel, hence avoiding one of the down sides of multiple-choice hashing.

5.4.2 GETTING DATA IN AND OUT

The design of *Glacier*, but also that of other FPGA-based stream processors, assumes that data can be consumed and produced in a particular format defined by the processing engine. For instance, *Glacier* assumes that data arrives as a parallel set of wires, with a data_valid signal indicating the presence of data (see Section 5.4.1) and the same data format is produced as the engine's output.

Thus, to interface with application-level stream formats, *glue logic* must be placed around hardware query plans and translate between formats:

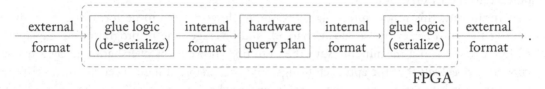

Incoming data is being de-serialized to the internal format of the hardware execution plan. The produced query output is brought into an external wire format before it leaves the FPGA chip again.

Observe how glue logic usually requires some additional chip area. Interfacing with outside data formats does not, however, usually lead to a noticeable runtime overhead on the query processing task. Assuming that glue logic components can keep up with the stream data rates, they cooperate with the hardware plan in a pipelining fashion. The additional latency (order of a few FPGA cycles) is typically negligible.

Implementing a de-serialization component can be a tedious task. Conceptually, it resembles the writing of a software parser. But unlike in the software world, very few tools (such as (f)lex or JLex for C/Java) exist to generate hardware parsers from high-level language specifications. One tool to generate VHDL code from regular language grammars is *Snowfall* [Teubner and Woods, 2011]. Similar in spirit to compiler generators for software parsers, *Snowfall* allows a grammar specification to be annotated with *action code*. At runtime, this action code may, for instance, drive signal wires depending on the syntactical structure of the input stream.

As in the software domain, serializing the output of a query processor into an application format usually amounts to a sequential program (implemented via a small, sequential state machine) that emits field values as required by the format.

5.5 DYNAMIC QUERY WORKLOADS

All of the systems and strategies discussed above assume a processing model that is illustrated in Figure 5.16 (assuming the *Glacier* query compiler). In this model, a query compiler generates a description for a dedicated hardware circuit (e.g., using VHDL) that implements the input query.

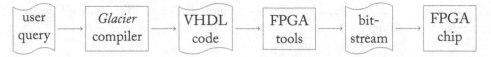

Figure 5.16: Processing model for FPGA-accelerated query processing. A query-to-hardware compiler (e.g., *Glacier*) compiles the user query into a circuit description. Standard FPGA design tools generate a bitstream from that, which is uploaded to the FPGA chip.

FPGA design tools, such as Xilinx ISE convert this description into a runnable bitstream that is uploaded to the FPGA for execution.

Intuitively, this model offers high flexibility, allows maximum performance (by fully re-tailoring the chip for every workload change), and leverages the re-programming capabilities of FPGA devices in a meaningful way. This intuition, however, is overshadowed by a massive *compilation overhead* that the approach brings. The conversion of high-level circuit descriptions into a runnable bitstream is highly compute intensive; the vpr program in the SPEC CPU2000 benchmark suite even uses the place & route task to measure CPU performance. By comparison, compilation to VHDL and re-configuration of the FPGA can be performed quickly.[5]

5.5.1   FAST WORKLOAD CHANGES THROUGH PARTIAL MODULES

A countermeasure for high circuit compilation cost was suggested by Dennl et al. [2012] and applied to a *Glacier*-like scenario. The idea is to build hardware execution plans from a set of hard-wired components, but composing and wiring them in flexible ways, tailored to the particular user query at hand. To this end, all components adhere to a very strict port interface, so arbitrary components can be mixed and matched as needed.

Interfacing Between Components.   The wiring interface used in *Glacier*, illustrated in Figure 5.13, is *not* suited for such a use. The width of the tuple data part of this interface depends on the schema of the (sub-)expression q. If turned into generic components, those would have to have a fixed tuple width. Limited chip resources rule out straightforward workarounds, such as over-provisioning the wiring interface for very wide tuples.

Dennl et al. [2012] thus forward tuple data in chunks of fixed size (which is chosen to match the processing word width). That is, tuples $t_i = \langle a_i, b_i, c_i, d_i \rangle$ are pushed through the series of

---

[5]The latter is only bottlenecked by a limited configuration bus bandwidth, which can be mitigated, e.g., by compressing the bitstream before uploading it to the chip [Li and Hauck, 2001]. Multi-context FPGA devices offer a double buffering mechanism for configuration; Tabula's "3d programmable logic devices" allow us to switch between configurations at multi-gigahertz rates [Tabula, Inc., 2010].

processing components in a pipeline fashion:

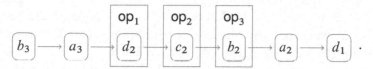

(The illustration assumes an execution plan of three operators. The first of them is just seeing the last attribute of tuple t_2.) In this representation, the port width between neighboring components is constant and tuples of arbitrary width could be processed.

Configuring Modules.   Minimal compilation cost is achieved by using pre-compiled modules to instantiate the op_i in the above illustration. To guarantee the necessary flexibility, most modules will be generic operators that can be parameterized to fit the particular operator requirements and the given input/output tuple schemata. In the implementation of Dennl et al. [2012], configuration parameters are communicated over the same data path as the payload data. Additional handshake signals ensure that both uses are handled as appropriate.

A particular configuration parameter are tuple field names where hardware operators read their input from or, equivalently, the *chunk index* where the respective field can be found within the input stream. For operator results (e.g., the outcome of an arithmetic or Boolean operation), Dennl et al. [2012] use an in-band transfer mechanism; results are simply written into available chunks of the data stream. To make this possible, the input data stream is interspersed with *spare chunks* that can be used for that purpose.

Runtime Reconfiguration.   Once the interfaces between hardware components are fixed, the "mix & match" idea of Dennl et al. [2012] may even be used in combination with *partial reconfiguration*. With some restrictions, this feature of modern FPGA chips allows us to swap sub-circuits of a larger hardware design in and out at runtime. Such a strategy is best suited if multiple queries are run concurrently on a single FPGA chip. Queries can then be added/removed from the chip without a need to stop running queries for the reconfiguration.

The price to pay for the partial reconfiguration capability is that the size of all components must fit the granularity of a reconfiguration frame (a device-specific value; 20/40 configurable logic blocks for Xilinx Virtex-5/6 devices). According to Dennl et al. [2012], this overhead is bearable and amounts to about 30 % lost chip space.

5.6   BIBLIOGRAPHIC NOTES

FPGAs have been used for regular expression matching in a number of scenarios. Clark and Schimmel [2004] suggested their use for network packet analysis. Mitra et al. [2009] showed how XML publish/subscribe systems could be accelerated with FPGA-based pattern matching. Later, they refined their approach to handle a larger class of twig-based XML patterns [Moussalli et al., 2011]. Sadoghi et al. [2011] used FPGAs for a very similar application scenario, but their system is not based on state automata and regular expression matching. Rather, they break down their input data into attribute/value pairs and match them through their "Propagation" algorithm.

Vaidya et al. [2010] extended the Borealis stream processing engine [Abadi et al., 2005] and accelerated a use case where traffic information obtained through a video channel is pre-processed using dedicated image processing logic on the FPGA. The design of this *Symbiote* system is such that partial or entire plan trees can be migrated to the FPGA or handled on the CPU.

The data path concept of Section 5.3 resembles the idea of *database machines*. In this line of research, various groups built special-purpose hardware that could pre-filter data as it is being read from persistent storage. Most notable here is the DIRECT engine of DeWitt [1979].

Outside the database and stream processing world, researchers have very successfully used FPGAs in, e.g., scientific applications. The use of FGPAs at CERN's Large Hadron Collider (LHC) essentially follows the data path architecture that we looked at on page 61. Data rates of several terabits per second, produced by the particle accelerator, are way above what could be processed and archived on commodity hardware. Thus, FPGA-based *triggers* pre-analyze the high-volume input stream, so only relevant information gets forwarded to the main processing flow. Gregerson et al. [2009] illustrate this for (parts of) the Compact Muon Solenoid (CMS) Trigger at CERN. There, an FPGA-based filter reduces a 3 Tb/s input stream to manageable 100 Mb/s.

CHAPTER 6

Accelerated DB Operators

In the previous chapter, we illustrated various ways of applying FPGAs to stream processing applications. In this chapter, we illustrate that FPGAs also have the potential to accelerate more classical data processing tasks by exploiting various forms of parallelism inherent to FPGAs. In particular, we will discuss FPGA-acceleration for two different database operators *(i)* sort and *(ii)* skyline.

6.1 SORT OPERATOR

Sorting is a fundamental operation in any database management system. Various other database operators such as joins or GROUP BY aggregation can be implemented efficiently when input tuples to these operators are sorted. However, sorting is a rather expensive operation that can easily become the bottleneck in a query plan. Hence, accelerating sorting can have great impact on overall query processing performance in a database. In this section, we will discuss a number of different approaches to sort small as well as large problem sets with FPGAs.

6.1.1 SORTING NETWORKS

We will start this chapter with a simple example, where only very small data sets are sorted in hardware, consisting of, say, only eight values. Mueller et al. [2012] investigated how to do this on FPGAs using so-called *sorting networks*. This example will underline once more the fundamental differences of laying out an algorithm in hardware versus executing a corresponding software program on a microprocessor.

The key idea of sorting networks is to stream unsorted data through a series of *compare-and-swap* elements, as the one illustrated on the right. This will bring the data into the desired sort order. The compare-and-swap element is constructed from a 32-bit comparator, which drives two cross-coupled 32-bit multiplexers, i.e., if input *B* is smaller than input *A* both multiplexers will select the other value and hence the values will be swapped.

In Figure 6.1, eighteen such *compare-and-swap* elements (illustrated as ⦙) are combined to form an eight-way sorting network. We display the new values on the wires in gray whenever

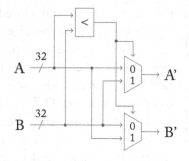

a swap happens, e.g., at the first stage four pairs of 32-bit wire buses with values (5,8), (3,1), (2,7), and (4,6) are processed in parallel and only the values of the third and fourth bus need to

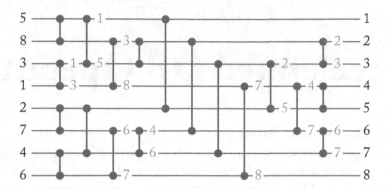

Figure 6.1: Eight-way *even-odd* sorting network using 18 *compare-and-swap* elements.

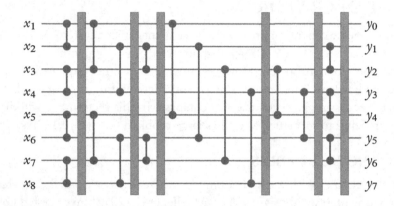

Figure 6.2: Fully pipelined even-odd sorting network with six pipeline stages.

be swapped: $(3,1) \rightarrow (1,3)$. After all values have propagated through all the compare-and-swap elements they appear in sorted order at the output of the circuit, i.e., the smallest value is at the topmost output and the largest value appears at the bottom output.

There are several ways that compare-and-swap elements can be arranged to build a sorting network. The arrangement shown here is known as *even-odd* sorting network. Mueller et al. [2012] also discuss other sorting networks in detail such as *bitonic* sorting networks or networks based on *bubble sort*. Different arrangements of the compare-and-swap elements mostly affect resource consumption and ease of implementation, and we will not discuss them any further here.

One problem with the circuit depicted in Figure 6.1 is that the longest signal path has to traverse six compare-and-swap elements. The maximum clock frequency at which a circuit can be clocked is determined by the longest signal path of a circuit. By inserting *pipeline registers* into the circuit the longest signal path can be shortened. In Figure 6.2, we illustrate such pipeline registers

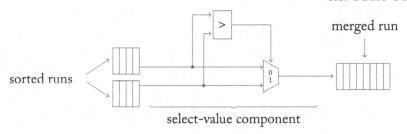

Figure 6.3: Select-value component merges two sorted runs into a larger sorted run.

with gray boxes. With the pipeline registers in place, every signal now only needs to traverse one compare-and-swap element to the next pipeline register. At every clock tick, intermediate states are stored in the pipeline registers, allowing the circuit to partially process six different data sets concurrently in six different stages.

Mueller et al. [2012] report that a similar pipelined circuit to the one shown in Figure 6.2 could be clocked at $f_{clk} = 267\,\text{MHz}$. Since the circuit processes 8×32 bits per clock cycle, a data processing rate of 8.5 GB/s was achieved. A sorting network with twice as many inputs (i.e., 16×32-bit words) at the same clock rate would double the throughput. However, it quickly becomes difficult to move data in and out of the FPGA at these high processing rates and the complexity of the sorting circuits exponentially increases with more inputs. Thus, sorting networks are a very efficient way to sort small sets of values that could be used, e.g., to implemented a hardware accelerated sort instruction of a closely coupled microprocessor to sort SIMD registers.

6.1.2   BRAM-BASED FIFO MERGE SORTER

The sorting network example of the previous section suggests a tightly coupled CPU/FPGA architecture, where the FPGA is invoked at the granularity of individual instructions. If we could off-load bigger chunks of data to be completely sorted by the FPGA, this would reduce communication between FPGA and CPU, and the CPU would have more time to take care of other tasks while the FPGA is sorting. Koch and Torresen [2011] proposed to use BRAM-based FIFO queues to implement a *merge sorter* that can efficiently sort larger problem sizes inside the FPGA.

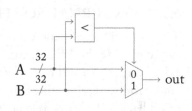

At the heart of the merge sorter a *select-value* component is used, which is illustrated on the right. The select-value component is half of the compare-and-swap component of the previous section, i.e., two values A and B are compared and the smaller one is *selected*. The select-value component can be used to merge two sorted runs into a larger sorted run, as depicted in Figure 6.3.

The inputs to the select-value component A and B are read from two FIFOs, where each FIFO stores a sorted run. The smaller of the two inputs is selected and written to an output

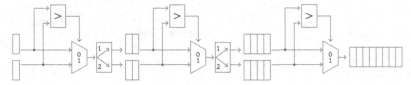

Figure 6.4: A cascade of FIFO merge sorters used to produce large sorted runs.

FIFO. Then the next value is requested from the input FIFO that has submitted the smaller value. Figure 6.4 shows how a cascade of such merge sorters can be combined to create larger and larger sorted runs. The output of the select-value component is directed to a first output FIFO until it is filled and then redirected to a second output FIFO. Those output FIFOs then serve as inputs to the next select-value component.

Koch and Torresen [2011] observed that at each stage, processing can start after the first input FIFO has been filled and the first value of the second FIFO arrives. Furthermore, the select-value component always only reads from one of the two input FIFOs and the result is written to only one of the two output FIFOs. Hence, the overall fill level of the FIFOs is constant. Therefore, the second FIFO is not strictly necessary. Koch and Torresen [2011] showed how to get rid of the second FIFO. To do so, however, they had to build a custom FIFO based on a linked list structure to deal with the two read and two write pointers within a single FIFO.

Koch and Torresen [2011] evaluated the FIFO merge sorter described above. Using 98% of the available BRAM it was possible to sort 43,000 64-bit keys (344 KB) in a single iteration, i.e., by streaming the keys through the FPGA once. The circuit could be clocked at $f_{clk} = 252\,\text{MHz}$ resulting in a throughput of 2 GB/s.

6.1.3   EXTERNAL SORTING WITH A TREE MERGE SORTER

To sort even bigger data sets that exceed the capacity of on-chip BRAM storage, runs need to be stored outside the FPGA, e.g., in DRAM on the FPGA card. Nevertheless, merging of several external runs can still be performed in a streaming manner inside the FPGA, i.e., as the FPGA reads from several smaller runs stored in DRAM, it can continuously write tuples of the merged result back to DRAM to generate larger runs, or back to the host (e.g., via PCI-Express) for the final run.

To merge several runs into one larger run a *merge sorter tree* can be used, e.g., as the one illustrated in Figure 6.5 on the left, which merges eight runs. The tree is constructed from several *select-value* components, represented by the gray boxes in the figure. DRAM latency can be hidden by placing small FIFOs between the tree and external memory. A load unit then monitors the fill-level of all FIFOs and coordinates DRAM read requests accordingly. To avoid clock speed degradation, large merge sorter trees need to be pipelined, e.g., by adding tiny FIFOs between every level of the tree.

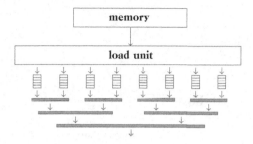 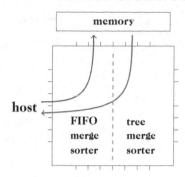

Figure 6.5: Tree merge sorter (left), and a combination of a FIFO merge sorter with a tree merge sorter connected to external DRAM (right).

On the right-hand-side of Figure 6.5 a combination of the FIFO merge sorter, described in the previous section, and a tree merge sorter is illustrated. In a first step, unsorted data is streamed through the FIFO merge sorter on the FPGA, which generates initial runs that are stored in external DRAM. Then these runs are read back from DRAM and merged by a tree merge sorter before the final result is sent back to the host. If the data set is so large that one pass through the tree merge sorter is not enough then multiple round trips to DRAM would be necessary.

Koch and Torresen [2011] report that the tree-merge-sorter achieved a throughput of 1 GB/s on their FPGA, and could merge up to 4.39 million keys (35.1 MB) in one pass. However, this measurement assumes that the entire FPGA can be used for merging. For a configuration like the one in Figure 6.5 on the right, where both a FIFO merge sorter and a tree merge sorter need to fit on the same FPGA 1,08 million keys (8.6 MB) could be sorted at a throughput of 1 GB/s.

6.1.4 SORTING WITH PARTIAL RECONFIGURATION

For a configuration as in Figure 6.5 on the right, where a *FIFO merge sorter* needs to share the available FPGA resources with a *tree merge sorter*, each module can only solve half the problem size per run. However, notice that the two modules do not run in parallel, i.e., first the FIFO merge sorter generates initial runs in DRAM, and once those runs are generated, they are merged by the tree merge sorter.

To increase device utilization, an alternative is to first use the entire FPGA for the FIFO merge sorter, and then use *dynamic partial reconfiguration* to load the tree merge sorter after the FIFO merge sorter has terminated, as illustrated in Figure 6.6.

With this approach, both the FIFO merge sorter and the tree merge sorter can sort larger problem sizes in one pass. However, the time required for reconfiguration needs to be considered

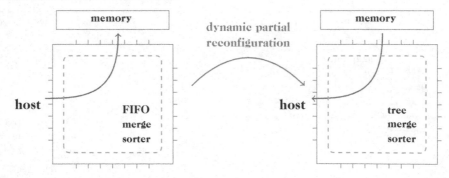

Figure 6.6: Using dynamic partial reconfiguration to first run the FIFO merge sorter and then the tree merge sorter in the same *partially reconfigurable region*.

as well. The configuration time of a partially reconfigurable region is directly proportional to its size. Koch and Torresen [2011] measured roughly 3 MB configuration data for the sorter modules. At a configuration speed of 400 MB/s, this means that during the time it takes to swap in the tree merge sorter module, the FIFO merge sorter module could have sorted 5×3 MB of data because of the five times higher throughput (2 GB/s).

Thus, dynamic partial reconfiguration only pays off for large problem sizes. For a sorting problem with 4 million keys Koch and Torresen [2011] measured a configuration overhead of 46 %, while for 448 million keys (3.58 GB) the configuration overhead is negligible. To sort this large data set, one run of the FIFO merge sorter and two runs of the tree merge sorter were necessary resulting in an overall throughput of 667 MB/s.

6.2   SKYLINE OPERATOR

Skyline queries compute the *Pareto-optimal* set of multi-dimensional data points. They are a good example of a complex database task that can greatly benefit from FPGA acceleration due to their compute-intensive nature, especially when dealing with higher dimensions. Formally, the *skyline* of a set of multi-dimensional data points is defined as follows:

Definition 6.1   A tuple t_i *dominates* ($\prec$) another tuple t_j iff every dimension of t_i is *better*[1] *than or equal to* the corresponding dimension of t_j and at least one dimension of t_i is *strictly better* than the corresponding dimension of t_j.

Definition 6.2   Given a set of input tuples $I = \{t_1, t_2, \ldots t_n\}$, the skyline query returns a set of tuples S, such that any tuple $t_i \in S$ is not *dominated* by any other tuple $t_j \in I$.

---

[1]Here, "better" means either smaller or larger depending on the query.

```
1   foreach tuple qᵢ ∈ queue do
2   |   isDominated = false;
3   |   foreach tuple pⱼ ∈ window do
4   |   |   if qᵢ.timestamp > pⱼ.timestamp then          /* pⱼ is part of the skyline */
5   |   |   |   output(pⱼ);
6   |   |   |   window.drop(pⱼ);
7   |   |   else if qᵢ ≺ pⱼ then                          /* pⱼ is dominated by qᵢ */
8   |   |   |   window.drop(pⱼ);
9   |   |   else if pⱼ ≺ qᵢ then                          /* qᵢ is dominated by pⱼ */
10  |   |   |   isDominated = true;
11  |   |   |   break;
12  |   if not isDominated then                          /* qᵢ is a potential skyline tuple */
13  |   |   timestamp(qᵢ);
14  |   |   if window.isFull() then                       /* add qᵢ to the window later */
15  |   |   |   queue.insert(qᵢ);
16  |   |   else                                          /* there is space in the window */
17  |   |   |   window.insert(qᵢ);
```

Figure 6.7: Standard Block Nested Loops (BNL) Algorithm ($\prec$ means "dominates").

6.2.1 STANDARD BLOCK NESTED LOOPS (BNL) ALGORITHM

FPGAs exhibit tremendous aggregated compute power but they can only keep a limited amount of state in the chip during computation, as we have already seen in Section 6.1. In the case of skyline queries, it is possible that the intermediate state or even the final result exceed the capacity of current FPGAs. Woods et al. [2013] implemented a highly parallel variant of the *block nested loops* (BNL) [Börzsönyi et al., 2001] algorithm on an FPGA. The BNL algorithm is appealing for an FPGA implementation because it was designed exactly for this scenario, although in a software context, where all data does not fit into main memory.

In Figure 6.7, the BNL algorithm is given in pseudocode. All input tuples are stored in a queue and then compared one by one against a window of w potential skyline tuples. If an input tuple is dominated by a potential window tuple, it is discarded. On the other hand, all window tuples that are dominated by an input tuple are removed from the window.

After an input tuple has been compared against all potential skyline tuples in the window, the input tuple itself is either inserted into the window as a potential skyline tuple (when there is room), or else it is inserted into the queue of input tuples again for later processing. In both cases, the tuple is timestamped. A potential window tuple p_i becomes a true skyline tuple when

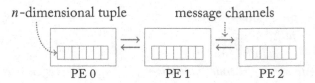

n-dimensional tuple   message channels

PE 0   PE 1   PE 2

Figure 6.8: Window tuples (consisting of several dimensions) are distributed over a pipeline of processing elements. Neighboring processing elements are connected via 32-bit message channels.

it either encounters the first tuple q_j from the input queue that has a larger timestamp or when the input queue is empty. A larger timestamp indicates that two tuples must have already been compared and since the queue is totally ordered, all following tuples in the queue will also have larger timestamps. The algorithm terminates when the input queue is empty.

6.2.2   PARALLEL BNL WITH FPGAS

In the FPGA implementation of Woods et al. [2013], the queue of input tuples is stored in DRAM mounted on an FPGA card, i.e., outside of the FPGA chip, and only the window of potential skyline tuples is maintained inside the FPGA. Result tuples (i.e., skyline tuples) are also written back to DRAM. Hence, input tuples are streamed from the DRAM through the FPGA and back to DRAM. Several iterations may be necessary until the algorithm terminates.

Pipeline of Processing Elements (PEs)

In BNL, each input tuple needs to be compared against all potential skyline tuples stored in the window. This is an expensive process since the window may consist of several hundred tuples. To achieve high throughput only a minimal number of clock cycles should be spent on each input tuple before the next tuple is read from the queue. Thus, Woods et al. [2013] propose to distribute the window of potential skyline tuples over a pipeline of daisy-chained processing elements, as illustrated in Figure 6.8.

A processing element stores a single tuple of the window. An input tuple is submitted to the first processing element in the pipeline from where it is forwarded to the neighboring processing element after evaluation via the specified message channel. Thus, w processing elements operate on the window concurrently such that w dominance tests are performed in parallel, where w is the size of the window.

Causality Guarantees

The processing elements are organized in a way that input tuples are evaluated in a strictly feed-forward oriented way. This has important consequences that can be exploited in order to parallelize the execution over many processing elements while preserving the causality of the corresponding sequential algorithm.

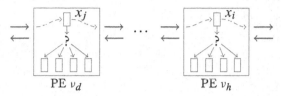

Figure 6.9: Causality guarantees. The earlier x_i will see no effects caused by the later x_j but x_j sees all effects of x_i.

Feed-forward processing implies that the global working set is scanned exactly once in a defined order. What is more, once an input tuple x_i has reached a processing element v_h, its evaluation cannot be affected by any later input tuple x_j that is evaluated over a preceding processing element v_d (conversely, the later x_j is guaranteed to see all effects caused by the earlier x_i).

These causality guarantees hold even if we let the executions of x_i on v_h and x_j on v_d run *in parallel* on independent compute resources, as illustrated in Figure 6.9. For example, once an input tuple x_i reaches the last processing element, it can safely be assumed that it has been compared against all other working set tuples and appropriate actions can be invoked.

Parallel BNL as Two-Phase Algorithm

In summary, the parallel version of BNL works as follows. Input tuples propagate through the pipeline of processing elements and are evaluated against a different window tuple at every stage in the pipeline. If at one point an input tuple is dominated, a flag is set that propagates through the pipeline together with every tuple. On the other hand, if a window tuple is dominated it is deleted. When an input tuple reaches the last processing element, and was not dominated by any window tuple (indicated by the domination flag), the tuple is timestamped and then inserted into the window if there is space, or written back to DRAM otherwise. Notice that new potential skyline tuples can only be inserted into the window at the last processing element to ensure that they have been compared to all existing window tuples. This means that free slots in the window that occur when window tuples are dominated need to propagate toward the end of the pipeline. To enforce this, neighboring processing elements can swap their contents.

The processing elements execute the algorithm just described in two phases: *(i)* an *evaluation phase* and *(ii)* a *shift phase*. During the *evaluation phase*, a new state is determined for each processing element; but these changes are not applied before the *shift phase*, which is the phase that allows nearest neighbor communication. Those two phases run synchronously across the FPGA, as depicted in Figure 6.10.

6.2.3   PERFORMANCE CHARACTERISTICS

In their evaluation, Woods et al. [2013] showed interesting performance characteristic of parallel BNL running on an FPGA. They evaluated their FPGA-based skyline operator against a

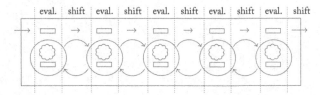

Figure 6.10: Two-phase processing in parallel BNL. Circles represent processing elements. A processing element consists of logic, storage for the window tuple, and communication channels to neighboring processing elements.

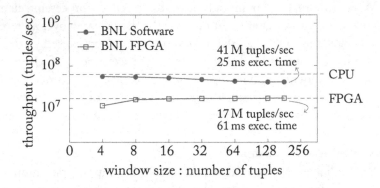

Figure 6.11: Correlated dimensions resulting in a small skyline. Performance is memory bound.

single-threaded software implementation, as well as a state-of-the-art multi-threaded skyline implementation [Park et al., 2009]. As we will discuss, the comparisons with the single-threaded software implementation (Figure 6.11 and Figure 6.12) highlight several fundamental differences between CPUs and FPGAs.

For their experiments, Woods et al. [2013] use data sets with common data distributions to evaluate skyline computation. Figure 6.11 shows the results for a data set, where the dimensions of the tuples are *correlated*. This means that the values in all dimensions of a tuple are similar resulting in very few skyline tuples that dominate all other tuples. As can been seen in the figure, both implementations achieve a throughput that is close to the maximum possible throughput given by the memory subsystem (dashed lines). The CPU achieves better performance here because it has the more efficient memory subsystem. The total number of dominance tests is very low, i.e., essentially what is measured is how fast main memory can be read/written on the given platform.

By contrast, the results displayed in Figure 6.12 for a data set where the dimensions of the tuples are *anti-correlated*, present the two implementations in a different light. Anti-correlated means that tuples with high values in some dimensions are likely to have low values in other

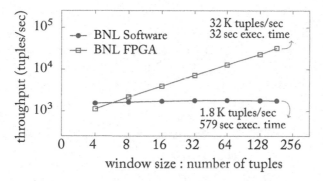

Figure 6.12: Anti-correlated dimensions resulting in a large skyline. Performance is compute bound.

dimensions, i.e., there are many incomparable tuples[2] leading to many dominance tests. Hence, skyline computation is now heavily compute-bound.

For the software variant, increasing the window size has little effect on throughput because the number of total dominance tests stays roughly the same independent of the window size. For the FPGA implementation, on the other hand, increasing the window means adding processing elements, i.e., compute resources, which is why throughput increases linearly with the window size.

Notice that the computation of the skyline for the anti-correlated data set is significantly more expensive, e.g., the best execution time of the CPU-based version has gone from 18 milliseconds to almost 10 minutes. This slowdown is due to the increased number of comparisons since all skyline tuples have to be pairwise compared with each other. Thus, the workloads where the FPGA excels are also the ones where acceleration is needed most.

As mentioned previously, Woods et al. [2013] also compared their implementation against *PSkyline* [Park et al., 2009], a state-of-the-art parallel skyline operator for multicores. The performance achieved with a low-end FPGA was comparable to the one of PSkyline on a 64-core Dell PowerEdge Server using 64 threads. However, notice that there is a significant difference in price (FPGA = $750 versus Dell = $12,000), as well as power consumption[3] between the two systems. Moreover, with 192 processing elements a throughput of 32,000 tuples/sec (anti-correlated distribution) is reached on the FPGA. This is more than two orders of magnitude below the upper bound of 17 million tuples/sec (cf. Figure 6.11), i.e., with a larger FPGA, there is still a lot of leeway to further increase performance by adding more processing elements.

---

[2]Two tuples are *incomparable* if neither tuple dominates the other one.
[3]FPGAs use between one and two orders of magnitude less power than CPUs.

CHAPTER 7

Secure Data Processing

So far, we have manly highlighted advantages of FPGAs with respect to performance, e.g., for low-latency and/or high-volume stream processing. An entirely different area where FPGAs provide a number of benefits is *secure data processing*. Especially in the cloud computing era, guaranteeing *data confidentiality*, *privacy*, etc., are increasingly important topics. In this chapter, we first compare FPGAs to CPUs and ASICs regarding security aspects before we describe a few key features of modern FPGAs that allow them to be used as even more secure co-processors. Finally, we discuss a use case—*Cipherbase*—a recent project that achieves *data confidentiality* in Microsoft's SQL Server using FPGAs.

7.1 FPGAS VERSUS CPUS

CPU-based systems are typically very complex, both in respect to hardware and software. This means that there are many possibilities for attacks, i.e., bugs in the operating system, the device drivers, the compiler, hardware components, etc., can all be exploited to attack the system, and as a result it is very difficult to make such systems secure. FPGAs have a much smaller attack surface.

7.1.1 VON NEUMANN ARCHITECTURE

Most CPU-based systems today are designed according to the *Von Neumann architecture*, i.e., data and executable code are stored in the same contiguous memory. This is a major security problem, allowing for various code injection attacks. On an FPGA, it is easy to *physically* separate data and program, i.e., a program can be implemented in logic, while data is stored in on-chip dedicated memory.

Another problem is isolating multiple applications from each other. Again, in an FPGA two applications could run in *physically* isolated regions of the FPGA, only sharing perhaps some I/O channel to which access can be granted in a secure manner. On a multicore CPU this is virtually impossible, i.e., even if two applications are executed on different cores, those cores will still share a lot of resources such as caches, memory, I/O devices, etc.

7.1.2 TRUSTED PLATFORM MODULE (TPM)

There have been numerous attempts in the past to make CPU-based software systems more secure. For instance, the *Trusted Platform Module* (TPM) chip is a secure cryptoprocessor that can store cryptographic keys. Together with the BIOS, the TPM chip provides a *"root of trust"* that can be used for *authenticated boot*. However, one limitation of this approach is that while software is authenticated when loaded, there is no protection against modification of the code at runtime. Circuits running on an FPGA are much more difficult to tamper with, especially if the security features that we will discuss in Section 7.3 are enabled.

Another limitation is that the TPM chip cannot do encryption/decryption on its own. It can only transfer the cryptographic keys to a region in memory, which the BIOS is supposed to protect. Encryption/decryption are then performed by the processor. However, the BIOS cannot always protect main memory, e.g., with physical access to a computer an attacker can retrieve the encryption keys from a running operating system with a so-called *cold boot attack*. This is an attack that relies on the fact that DRAM contents are still readable for a short period of time after power supply has been removed. In Section 7.4, we will discuss how FPGAs can be used as secure cryptoprocessors capable of encrypting/decrypting data, such that plaintext data never leave the chip.

7.2   FPGAS VERSUS ASICS

With respect to protecting intellectual property, FPGAs have an important advantage over ASICs. If circuit designer and circuit manufacturer are two different parties, then the designer needs to provide the manufacturer with the sensitive circuit description. In fact, very few companies such as Samsung or IBM design circuits and also own high-end semiconductor foundries to produce them. Most semiconductor companies are *fabless*. FPGAs allow a company to benefit from the latest manufacturing technology while keeping their circuit designs fully confidential.

Another threat to which ASICs are susceptible is *destructive analysis*, where each layer of the device is captured to determine its functionality. This technique is not applicable to determining the functionality of the circuit loaded onto an FPGA since the entire circuit specification is stored in on-chip configuration memory, i.e., there are no physical wires and gates of such a circuit that can be analyzed.

While circuits running on FPGAs are better protected than ASICs against reverse engineering threats as the ones described above, FPGAs exhibit other vulnerabilities. For example, by intercepting the bitstream during configuration of an FPGA the design could relatively easily be cloned or tampered with. In the next section, we discuss common mechanisms that guard FPGAs from such and other attacks.

7.3   SECURITY PROPERTIES OF FPGAS

FPGAs provide a number of security features to protect intellectual property (i.e., the circuit specification uploaded to the FPGA) from *reverse engineering*, *tampering*, and *counterfeiting*. In this section, we highlight the most important security-related features of modern FPGAs.

7.3.1   BITSTREAM ENCRYPTION

A number of FPGAs ship with an on-chip decryption engine to support *encrypted* bitstreams. Typically, the *advanced encryption standard* (AES) is implemented, which is a state-of-the art block cipher. The software that generates the bitstream also encrypts it before sending it to the FPGA. The FPGA then decrypts the bitstream on the chip before it writes the configuration to the corresponding locations. The key used for decryption is loaded into the FPGA once via the JTAG port, i.e., physical access to the FPGA is required. Then the key is stored using either on-chip (battery-backed) memory or non-volatile key storage such as OTP fuses. Hence, turning off power will not erase the key. Bitstream encryption ensures the *confidentiality* of a circuit design, preventing *reverse engineering* and device *cloning*.

7.3.2   BITSTREAM AUTHENTICATION

Besides bitstream encryption, Xilinx also introduced bitstream *authentication* with their Virtex-6 series. Thus, an on-chip keyed-HMAC algorithm implemented in hardware ensures that only authenticated users can modify an existing configuration or overwrite it with a different bitstream. During bitstream generation a *message authentication code* (MAC) is generated and embedded in the encrypted bitstream together with the HMAC key. During device configuration the MAC is recomputed on the FPGA using the provided HMAC key. In case the MAC computed by the FPGA does not match the MAC provided in the encrypted bitstream there are two options: either a fall-back bitstream is loaded or the configuration logic is disabled all together. HMAC ensures that the bitstream loaded into the FPGA has not been altered, preventing *tampering* of the bitstream, i.e., even single bit flips are detected. This protects an application running on an FPGA from attacks such as *spoofing* and *trojan horse attacks*.

7.3.3   FURTHER SECURITY MECHANISMS

Besides bitstream *encryption* and *authentication* FPGAs incorporate several other security mechanisms to guard against different kinds of attacks. For instance, the JTAG port—intended for device configuration and debugging—could be misused to reverse engineer the functionality of a specific design. Therefore, access to the JTAG port is usually highly restricted. In general, dedicated logic ensures that configuration memory cannot be read back via any external interface including the JTAG interface.

Some FPGA vendors go even one step further and continuously compute a CRC of the configuration data in the background, which is used to verify that no bits of configuration data have changed. A bit flip in the configuration data could be caused by a so-called *single-event upset* due to the impact of a high-energy neutron. Thus, monitoring the CRC of configuration data on a regular basis even allows detecting highly sophisticated *side channel* attacks at runtime.

7.4   FPGA AS TRUSTED HARDWARE

The *Cipherbase* system [Arasu et al., 2013] extends Microsoft's SQL Server with customized trusted hardware built using FPGAs. The project targets *data confidentiality* in the cloud. Cloud computing offers several advantages that make it attractive for companies to outsource data processing to the cloud. However, a major concern is processing *sensitive data*. Companies might not trust a cloud provider to keep their data confidential. In fact, in some cases a company might even want to protect highly confidential data from its own employees.

7.4.1   FULLY HOMOMORPHIC ENCRYPTION WITH FPGAS

Fully homomorphic encryption [Gentry, 2010] is a way to encrypt data such that certain types of computation can be executed directly on the ciphertext, i.e., without the need to decrypt the ciphertext. For instance, addition of two encrypted numbers would directly produce the encrypted result, i.e.:

$$Decrypt(Encrypt(A) + Encrypt(B)) = A + B$$

Since a program would never need to decrypt the data it is processing, fully homomorphic encryption would allow to safely execute computations on encrypted data in an untrusted environment. Unfortunately, fully homomorphic encryption is prohibitively expensive in practice [Bajaj and Sion, 2011].

In Cipherbase, fully homomorphic encryption is *simulated* by integrating closely coupled, trusted hardware into an untrusted system. Cipherbase considers an FPGA as a trusted black box that can compute a number of operations on data that are encrypted using a non-homomorphic encryption scheme such as AES (advanced encryption standard). That is, the FPGA actually decrypts data internally, computes the operation, and encrypts the result again before it leaves the trusted hardware, as illustrated below:

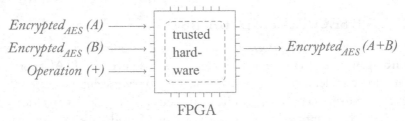

7.4.2   HYBRID DATA PROCESSING

In Cipherbase, the FPGA that implements the trusted cryptoprocessor is connected to the host server (running MS SQL Server) via PCI Express. The bandwidth of the PCI Express bus is lower than the bandwidth of the server's memory system, i.e., a performance penalty is associated with using the trusted cryptoprocessor. Therefore, a design goal of Cipherbase is to minimize data transfers between host and FPGA, and to do as little computation on the FPGA as possible to meet given security constraints.

Table 7.1: Typical plaintext operations and corresponding primitives to execute the same operations on ciphertext via FPGA.

Plaintext Operation	Primitive(s) executed on FPGA
$\sigma_{A=5}$	$Dec(\{A\}_{AES}) = Dec(\{5\}_{AES})$
π_{A+B}	$Enc(Dec(\{A\}_{AES}) + Dec(\{B\}_{AES}))$
$\bowtie_{A=B}^{hash}$	$Hash(Dec(\{A\}_{AES}));\ Dec(\{A\}_{AES}) = Dec(\{B\}_{AES})$
$\text{sum}(B)$	$Enc(Dec(\{B\}_{AES}) + Dec(\{partial sum\}_{AES}))$
Index lookup	$FindPos(Dec(\{k\}_{AES}), \langle Dec(\{k_1\}_{AES}), \dots, Dec(\{k_n\}_{AES})\rangle)$
Range lock	$Dec(\{v\}_{AES}) \in [Dec(\{l\}_{AES}), Dec(\{h\}_{AES})]$

We can distinguish several forms of *hybrid data processing* in Cipherbase, meaning that some parts of the processing are handled on commodity hardware while other parts are executed in the secure environment on the FPGA. First of all, users can specify the level of confidentiality guarantees at a column granularity. For example, when processing employee records, the "salary" field might require strong confidentiality guarantees while "employer address" might not. Hence, columns and tables that have no confidentiality restrictions will not be processed by the trusted hardware, allowing for a more efficient execution.

Furthermore, even individual operators can be broken down into the parts that need to be executed by the cryptoprocessor and others that can be handled unprotected by the standard database software. For instance, consider (B-tree) index processing, where a confidential column is indexed. Searching within an index page requires decrypting confidential keys, i.e., needs to be executed by the cryptoprocessor. On the other hand, many other index operations such as concurrency control, buffer pool management, recovery, etc., can be handled outside the crpytoprocesor.

Since FPGA and host system are tightly coupled, a few primitives (cf. Table 7.1) that can be called from the host system and are implemented on the FPGA are sufficient to extend a complete database system to support fully homomorphic encryption, as described above. Table 7.1 shows how primitives for decryption ($Dec(\cdot)$), encryption ($Enc(\cdot)$), and expression evaluation are invoked by the host system to execute a given operation on encrypted data.[1] Coming back to our index processing example, for each index page the $FindPos(\cdot)$ primitive would be called to determine the next page to visit. All other indexing logic—with the exception of checking key range locks[2]—can be handled by the standard database software running on the host.

---

[1]Encrypted data are denoted $\{\dots\}_{AES}$ assuming an AES encryption scheme.
[2]To check range locks another primitive needs to be invoked: $Dec(\{v\}_{AES}) \in [Dec(\{l\}_{AES}), Dec(\{h\}_{AES})]$.

Table 7.2: Stack machine for the expression $Dec(\{\$0\}_{AES}) = Dec(\{\$1\}_{AES})$.

Id	Instruction
1	GetData $0
2	Decrypt
3	GetData $1
4	Decrypt
5	Compare

7.4.3 TRUSTED HARDWARE IMPLEMENTATION

In Cipherbase, the main reason to use FPGAs is *security* rather than *performance*, i.e., *expressiveness* and *simplicity* are more important goals than speed of execution. On an FPGA, there is always a trade-off between expressiveness and performance. In Cipherbase it is of utmost importance that the system is *complete*. Notice that expressions in a projection, for instance, can be arbitrarily complex. Hence, to support all possible SQL queries the trusted hardware engine was designed as a *stack machine*, i.e., a restricted, special-purpose processor that runs inside the FPGA. The stack machine can execute a number of special instructions (e.g., for encryption, decryption, etc.), where each one is directly implemented in hardware.

When a query is compiled by the modified MS SQL Server, code is generated for the stack machine that runs on the FPGA. Each instruction is directly implemented in hardware and only parameters can be supplied at runtime. An example is given in Table 7.2, where the stack machine code is shown that evaluates a restriction expression of the form $Dec(\{\$0\}_{AES}) = Dec(\{\$1\}_{AES})$ on encrypted data. The compiler generates a sequence of instructions, of which some can have parameters (e.g., $0 and $1 in the example represent parameters).

The mechanisms described so far ensure that decrypted data never leave the FPGA. Nevertheless, access patterns are not hidden. While for many applications this is acceptable, Cipherbase also introduces the notion of *oblivious* operators that even hide data access patterns for applications that require a higher degree of confidentiality. It is beyond the scope of this book to discuss oblivious operators, and we therefore refer to the work of Arasu et al. [2013], Goodrich [2011] for a thorough discussion of the topic.

CHAPTER 8

Conclusions

Almost 50 years have passed since Gordon Moore observed that the number of transistors per integrated chip would double approximately every 2 years. Throughout these years, hardware technology followed the exponential growth with remarkable precision, and there is no indication that the trend will change any time soon.

The consequences of *Moore's Law* on chip technology, however, have changed dramatically over time. As already sketched in Chapter 1, *Moore's Law*—in combination with *Dennard scaling*—allowed to drive up clock frequencies and micro-architecture sophistication for many years. Power constraints set an end to this approach some ten years ago and hardware designers started to focus on *multi-core architectures* instead: additional transistors offered by *Moore's Law* were now turned into replicated on-chip processors ("cores").

Multi-core computing never *solved* the power consumption problem, however. At best, the now-prevalent way of leveraging hardware parallelism can be considered a temporary mechanism to mitigate the fundamental problem. A one-to-one conversion of Moore's dividend into additional CPU cores would incur an exponentially growing power consumption. But today's chips already operate at the limit in terms of heat dissipation and cooling.

POWER CONSTRAINTS AND DARK SILICON

Taylor [2012] discussed the search space for escapes to the urging power constraints and identified four basic strategies that he termed the *four horsemen of the coming dark silicon apocalypse*:

The Shrinking Horseman. Increased transistor densities could be used to reduce chip sizes—and thus cost—rather than to improve performance. The strategy does not per se offer a solution to the increased performance demand coming from the application side.

The Dim Horseman. An excess power budged from additional CPU cores can be avoided by *clocking down* all cores in the chip. Since power consumption grows super-linearly with the clock frequency, a chip with many low-frequency cores may be more power-efficient than the alternative of fewer high-frequency cores.

The Specialized Horseman. Rather than replicating the same core over and over, the chip could be populated with a diverse mix of processing units, each one (energy-)optimized for a particular task. Only few of these can be active together at any time (to meet the power budget). But hardware specialization will likely lead to a higher net energy efficiency.

The Deus Ex Machina Horseman. There might be an entirely unforeseen escape to the power limitation, e.g., by leveraging technologies other than the current MOSFET. However, waiting for miracles in the future can hardly be considered a strategy for problems that applications are suffering already today.

In this solution space, FPGAs could be considered a variation of the *specialized horseman*. But by contrast to the strategy in Taylor's narrow sense, an FPGA-based realization avoids the need to decide on a set of specialized units at chip design time. Rather, new or improved specialized units could be added to the portfolio of the system at any time. At the same time, no chip resources are "wasted" for specialized functionality that a particular system installation may never actually need (e.g., a machine purely used as a database server will hardly benefit from an on-chip H 264 video decoder).

FPGAS VS. ASICS

Reconfigurable hardware always comes at a price, however. In particular, a circuit realized in an FPGA will never be competitive with an implementation of the same functionality in dedicated custom hardware—neither in terms of raw performance, nor in terms of energy efficiency. Kuon and Rose [2007], for instance, quantified the penalty of reconfigurability to about 3× in performance and 14× in energy efficiency.

However, continuing integration densities will work more in favor of reconfigurable hardware than in favor of hard-wired alternatives, mainly for two reasons.

Reason 1: What to Specialize For?   As transistor count continues to increase, more and more tasks will have to be moved to specialized components (otherwise, technology will soon no longer benefit from Moore's Law again). The need to continuously specialize, however, will emphasize the challenge of deciding *what* to specialize for. As hardware moves toward specialized designs, the first specializations are rather easy to decide (for instance, a floating-point unit will benefit a wide range of applications at relatively little cost). But effectiveness will quickly wane for those specializations that come after. As mentioned before, this limitation will not arise in configurable hardware, since any application can instantiate just those accelerators that it actually can benefit from.

Reason 2: I/O Limitations   While available logic resources—for FPGAs as well as for ASICs— are expected to still grow exponentially for at least some more years, the number of *pins* per chip—and thus its *I/O capacity*—has been mostly stagnating for years already. This leads to a widening *I/O gap* between an increased compute capacity inside the chip and a lack of bandwidth to feed the logic with data.

Effectively, conventional circuits have growing difficulties to actually benefit from all their compute resources purely for bandwidth reasons (even if they were not constrained by energy). In such a situation, the better chip space efficiency of ASICs no longer provides an advantage over configurable hardware.

In summary, the fundamental FPGA technology—we sketched the combination of lookup tables and other components in Chapter 3—has been around for quite some time, but remained mostly a niche technology throughout most of this time. However, the conditions around the technology have changed only recently. ASIC technology is reaching limits (as discussed above), whereas today's FPGA chip sizes allows competitive functionality to be realized in configurable hardware.

OPEN CHALLENGES

Under these premises, we expect the relevance of FPGAs in computing systems to increase in the coming years. Hardware makers already demonstrated various ways to integrate configurable logic with commodity CPUs. Hybrid chips—where CPU(s) and configurable logic sit on the same die—are available today, commercially and at volume.

It is thus no longer a question whether or not FPGAs will appear in (mainstream) computing systems. Rather, the database community should begin to worry about how the potential of FPGAs can be *leveraged* to improve performance and/or energy efficiency.

Tools and Libraries   Several decades of research and development work have matured the software world to a degree that virtually any application field receives a rich set of support by tools, programming languages, libraries, but also design patterns and good practices. Hardware development is significantly more complex and has not yet reached the degree of convenience that software developers have long become used to.

FPGA development still has a rather steep learning curve and many software people shy away from the technology, because they cannot see the quick progress that they are used to from their home field. This is unfortunate not only because the potential of FPGA technology—once the entrance fee has been paid—is high, but also because hardware/software *co*-design has so far mostly been left to the hardware community. Clearly, the concept could benefit a lot from experience and technology (e.g., in software compilers, to name just one) that have become ubiquitous in the software world.

Systems Architectures   As discussed in Chapter 4, the final word on what is the best *system architecture* for hybrid CPU/FPGA processing has not yet been spoken. Moreover, data processing engines would likely benefit also from even more classes of modern system technology, including graphics processors (GPUs), massively parallel processor arrays (MPPAs) [Butts, 2007], or smart memories [Mai et al., 2000]. However, only small spots in the large space of possible system architectures have been explored, yet.

Finding a system architecture that brings together the potential of hardware and the requirements of (database) applications requires a fair amount of experimentation, systems building, and evaluation. Early results—some of which we also sketched in this book—are promising. But they also still show rough edges that need to be ironed out before they become attractive for practical use.

FPGAs as a Technology Enabler   Specialization and the use of FPGAs is often seen as a mechanism to improve quantitative properties of a data processing engine, e.g., its throughput, its latency, or its energy efficiency.

In Chapter 7, we showed that there are also scenarios where FPGAs can act as an *enabler* for functionality that cannot be matched with commodity hardware. With their outstanding flexibility, FPGAs might serve as an enabler also in further ways. For instance, placing configurable logic into the network fabric or near storage modules might open new opportunities that cannot be realized by conventional means.

Flexibility vs. Performance   In Chapter 4, we discussed trade-offs between runtime performance, flexibility, and re-configuration speed in FPGA designs. Circuit and systems design in general face very similar trade-offs.

General-purpose CPUs were always designed for *flexibility*, with application performance or energy efficiency only as secondary goals. These priorities are necessary with a technology and a market where one size *must* fit all.

Designers of FPGA circuits, however, are not bound to this prioritization. Rather, their circuit typically has to support just one very specific application type and the circuit can be re-built whenever it is no longer adequate for the current application load. And specialization usually yields sufficient performance advantages, so a "slow path" (e.g., using a general-purpose processor) for exceptional situations will not seriously affect performance.

Given this freedom to re-decide on trade-offs, it is really not clear which point in the design space should be chosen for a particular use case. As we already discussed in Chapter 4, existing research mostly explored configurations with fairly extreme decisions. We think, however, that the true potential of FPGA lies in the open space in-between. Most likely, the sweet spot is when different processing units, composed of one or more FPGA units; one or more general-purpose CPUs; and potentially even more units, operate together in the form of a *hybrid system design*.

APPENDIX A

Commercial FPGA Cards

Most commonly, FPGAs are mounted onto PCI Express plug-in cards. These cards are tailored at specific purposes (e.g., networking) but usually also have some general purpose extension slots to support pluggable daughter cards that can directly interface with the high-speed I/O transceivers of the FPGA.

A.1 NETFPGA

The NetFPGA project originated at Stanford University in 2007. It is an open source hardware and software platform targeted at networking research. The first generation development platform is called NetFPGA-1G. It is a PCI card with a Xilinx Virtex-II FPGA and a 4×1 Gbps networking interface. NetFPGA-10G is the latest development platform. Besides a much more powerful Xilinx Virtex-5 FPGA it also provides significantly more bandwidth, e.g., 40 Gigabit per second network bandwidth (4×10 Gbps Ethernet ports), and theoretical 4 Gigabyte per second maximum (bi-directional) PCI Express bandwidth (8 lanes, PCIe 2.0, 500MB/s per lane).

Network data are routed via high-speed I/O transceivers directly into the FPGA chip, where it can be processed at full *line-rate* without dropping packets, etc., making these cards very attractive for a variety of networking applications ranging from switches and routers to content processing applications such as deep packet inspection and network intrusion detection. The NetFPGA project is the only one of its kind, in the sense that it supports an active community of hardware and software developers that contribute to the project in the form of open source IP cores and reference designs. This significantly increases productivity for other developers.

NetFPGA has been successful also for commercial use, however. In particular, Algo-Logic, a US-based company, utilizes NetFPGA for applications in the area of low-latency trading applications [Lockwood et al., 2012].

A.2 SOLARFLARE'S APPLICATIONONLOAD™ ENGINE

Solarflare is one of the leading suppliers of low-latency Ethernet. The company provides 10 Gigabit Ethernet adapters, primarily targeting the financial markets. Recently, Solarflare has launched a new product—the ApplicationOnload™ Engine (AOE)—that combines one of their network interface cards (NICs) with an Altera Stratix V (GX A5) FPGA. The AOE (SFA6902F) provides two 10 Gbps Ethernet ports, PCI Express (8 lanes, PCIe 2.0, 500MB/s per lane), and four SODIMM DDR3 memory sockets (supporting up to 16 GB each). Form a hardware perspective, Solarflare's AOE and the NetFPGA are conceptually similar, however, the focus is different. While NetFPGA is a very FPGA-centric project, in Solarflare's AOE the FPGA is added to an existing product as a "bump-in-the-wire" co-processor. That is, the existing software stack for Solarfalre's NICs still runs on AOE, and only users with extreme performance demands, say for high-frequency trading, will start moving parts of the application into the FPGA on the NIC. This makes the transition to an FPGA-based system very smooth.

A.3   FUSION I/O'S IODRIVE

Fusion I/O operates in the PCIe SSD market. Solid state drives (SSDs) access flash storage via SATA/SAS interface, which were designed for hard disk access. Fusion I/O's ioDrive cards allow direct access to a flash memory storage tier via PCI Express, offering lower latency and better overall performance than commodity SSDs. Since Fusion I/O is a young company with a revolutionary product, they decided to implement the flash controller on the ioDrive card using an FPGA, rather than an ASIC. This allows the company to easily modify the controller, and provide "hardware-updates" to their customers. However, notice that here the FPGA really is a means to an end, i.e., ioDrive is a pure storage solution, and it is not intended that users program the FPGA themselves.

Bibliography

Daniel J. Abadi, Yanif Ahmad, Magdalena Balazinska, Ugur Çetintemel, Mitch Cherniack, Jeong-Hyon Hwang, Wolfgang Lindner, Anurag Maskey, Alex Rasin, Esther Ryvkina, Nesime Tatbul, Ying Xing, and Stanley B. Zdonik. The design of the Borealis stream processing engine. In *Proc. 2nd Biennial Conf. on Innovative Data Systems Research*, pages 277–289, January 2005. 70

Arvind Arasu, Spyros Blanas, Ken Eguro, Raghav Kaushik, Donald Kossmann, Ravi Ramamurthy, and Ramaratnam Venkatesan. Orthogonal security with Cipherbase. In *Proc. 6th Biennial Conf. on Innovative Data Systems Research*, January 2013. 7, 86, 88

Joshua Auerbach, David F. Bacon, Ioana Burcea, Perry Cheng, Stephen J. Fink, Rodric Rabbah, and Sunil Shukla. A compiler and runtime for heterogeneous computing. In *Proc. 49th Design Automaton Conference*, pages 271–276, June 2012. DOI: 10.1145/2228360.2228411 40

Sumeet Bajaj and Radu Sion. Trusteddb: a trusted hardware based database with privacy and data confidentiality. In *Proc. ACM SIGMOD Int. Conf. on Management of Data*, pages 205–216, June 2011. DOI: 10.1145/1989323.1989346 86

Zoran Basich and Emily Maltby. Looking for the 'next big thing'? ranking the top 50 start-ups. *The Wall Street Journal*, September 2012. 32

Stephan Börzsönyi, Donald Kossmann, and Konrad Stocker. The skyline operator. In *Proc. 17th Int. Conf. on Data Engineering*, 2001. DOI: 10.1109/ICDE.2001.914855 77

Mike Butts. Synchronization through communication in a massively parallel processor array. *IEEE Micro*, 27(5):32–40, September 2007. DOI: 10.1109/MM.2007.4378781 91

Christopher R. Clark and David E. Schimmel. Scalable pattern matching for high speed networks. In *Proc. 12th IEEE Symp. on Field-Programmable Custom Computing Machines*, pages 249–257, April 2004. DOI: 10.1109/FCCM.2004.50 69

Graham Cormode and Marios Hadjieleftheriou. Finding frequent items in data streams. *Proc. VLDB Endowment*, 1(2):1530–1541, 2008. DOI: 10.1007/3-540-45465-9_59 46

NVIDIA Corp. NVIDIA's next generation CUDA™ compute architecture: Kepler™ GK110, 2012. White Paper; version 1.0. 49

Sudipto Das, Shyam Antony, Divyakant Agrawal, and Amr El Abbadi. Thread cooperation in multicore architectures for frequency counting over multiple data streams. *Proc. VLDB Endowment*, 2(1):217–228, August 2009. 46

Jeffrey Dean and Sanjay Ghemawat. MapReduce: Simplified data processing on large clusters. In *Proc. 6th USENIX Symp. on Operating System Design and Implementation*, pages 137–150, December 2004. DOI: 10.1145/1327452.1327492 42

R.H. Dennard, F.H. Gaensslen, V.L. Rideout, E. Bassous, and A.R. LeBlanc. Design of ion-implanted mosfet's with very small physical dimensions. *Solid-State Circuits, IEEE Journal of*, 9(5):256–268, October 1974. DOI: 10.1109/JSSC.1974.1050511 1

Christopher Dennl, Daniel Ziener, and Jürgen Teich. On-the-fly composition of FPGA-based SQL query accelerators using a partially reconfigurable module library. In *Proc. 20th IEEE Symp. on Field-Programmable Custom Computing Machines*, pages 45–52, May 2012. DOI: 10.1109/FCCM.2012.18 35, 68, 69

David J. DeWitt. DIRECT—a multiprocessor organization for supporting relational database management systems. *IEEE Trans. Comput.*, c-28(6):182–189, June 1979. DOI: 10.1109/TC.1979.1675379 70

Hadi Esmaeilzadeh, Emily Blem, Renee St. Amant, Karthikeyan Sankaralingam, and Doug Burger. Dark silicon and the end of multicore scaling. In *Proc. 38th Annual Symp. on Computer Architecture*, pages 365–376, 2011. DOI: 10.1145/2024723.2000108 4

Robert W. Floyd and Jeffrey D. Ullman. The compilation of regular expressions into integrated circuits. *J. ACM*, 29(3):603–622, July 1982. DOI: 10.1145/322326.322327 54

Phil Francisco. The Netezza Data Appliance Architecture: A platform for high performance data warehousing and analytics. Technical Report REDP-4725-00, IBM Redguides, June 2011. 6, 36

Craig Gentry. Computing arbitrary functions of encrypted data. *Commun. ACM*, 53(3):97–105, March 2010. DOI: 10.1145/1666420.1666444 86

Michael T. Goodrich. Data-oblivious external-memory algorithms for the compaction, selection, and sorting of outsourced data. In *Proc. 23rd Annual ACM Symp. on Parallelism in Algorithms and Architectures*, June 2011. DOI: 10.1145/1989493.1989555 88

Naga K. Govindaraju, Brandon Lloyd, Wei Wang, Ming C. Lin, and Dinesh Manocha. Fast computation of database operations using graphics processors. In *Proc. ACM SIGMOD Int. Conf. on Management of Data*, pages 215–226, June 2004. DOI: 10.1145/1007568.1007594 49

Naga K. Govindaraju, Jim Gray, Ritesh Kumar, and Dinesh Manocha. GPUTeraSort: High performance graphics co-processor sorting for large database management. In *Proc. ACM SIGMOD Int. Conf. on Management of Data*, pages 325–336, June 2006. DOI: 10.1145/1142473.1142511 49

David J. Greaves and Satnam Singh. Kiwi: Synthesis of FPGA circuits from parallel programs. In *Proc. 16th IEEE Symp. on Field-Programmable Custom Computing Machines*, pages 3–12, April 2008. DOI: 10.1109/FCCM.2008.46 41

Anthony Gregerson, Amin Farmahini-Farahani, Ben Buchli, Steve Naumov, Michail Bachtis, Katherine Compton, Michael Schulte, Wesley H. Smith, and Sridhara Dasu. FPGA design analysis of the clustering algorithm for the CERN Large Hadron Collider. In *Proc. 17th IEEE Symp. on Field-Programmable Custom Computing Machines*, pages 19–26, 2009. DOI: 10.1109/FCCM.2009.33 70

Bingsheng He, Ke Yang, Rui Fang, Mian Lu, Naga K. Govindaraju, Qiong Luo, and Pedro V. Sander. Relational joins on graphics processors. In *Proc. ACM SIGMOD Int. Conf. on Management of Data*, pages 511–524, June 2008. DOI: 10.1145/1376616.1376670 49

Martin C. Herbordt, Yongfeng Gu, Tom VanCourt, Josh Model, Bharat Sukhwani, and Matt Chiu. Computing models for FPGA-based accelerators. *Computing in Science and Engineering*, 10(6):35–45, 2008. DOI: 10.1109/MCSE.2008.143 24

Mark D. Hill and Michael R. Marty. Amdahl's law in the multicore era. *IEEE Computer*, 41(7): 33–38, July 2008. DOI: 10.1109/MC.2008.209 3

Amir Hormati, Manjunath Kudlur, Scott A. Mahlke, David F. Bacon, and Rodric M. Rabbah. Optimus: Efficient realization of streaming applications on FPGAs. In *Proc. Int'l Conf. on Compilers, Architecture, and Synthesis for Embedded Systems*, pages 41–50, October 2008. DOI: 10.1145/1450095.1450105 40, 41

Intel Corp. The Intel® Xeon Phi™ coprocessor 5110P, 2012. Product Brief; more information at http://www.intel.com/xeonphi. 49

Hubert Kaeslin. *Digital Integrated Circuit Design*. Cambridge University Press, 2008. ISBN 978-0-521-88267-5. 44, 48

Adam Kirsch and Michael Mitzenmacher. The power of one move: Hashing schemes for hardware. *IEEE/ACM Transactions on Networking*, 18(6):1752–1765, December 2010. DOI: 10.1109/TNET.2010.2047868 66

Dirk Koch and Jim Torresen. FPGASort: A high performance sorting architecture exploiting run-time reconfiguration on FPGAs for large problem sorting. In *Proc. 19th ACM SIGDA Int. Symp. on Field Programmable Gate Arrays*, 2011. DOI: 10.1145/1950413.1950427 73, 74, 75, 76

Ian Kuon and Jonathan Rose. Measuring the gap between FPGAs and ASICs. *IEEE Trans. Computer-Aided Design of Integrated Circuits*, 26(2), February 2007. DOI: 10.1109/T-CAD.2006.884574 90

Zhiyuan Li and Scott Hauck. Configuration compression for Virtex FPGAs. In *Proc. 9th IEEE Symp. on Field-Programmable Custom Computing Machines*, pages 147–159, April 2001. DOI: 10.1109/FCCM.2001.19 68

John W. Lockwood, Adwait Gupte, Nishit Mehta, Michaela Blott, Tom English, and Kees Vissers. A low-latency library in FPGA hardware for high-frequency trading (HFT). In *IEEE 20th Annual Symp. on High-Performance Interconnects*, pages 9–16, August 2012. DOI: 10.1109/HOTI.2012.15 62, 93

Anil Madhavapeddy and Satnam Singh. Reconfigurable data processing for clouds. In *Proc. 19th IEEE Symp. on Field-Programmable Custom Computing Machines*, pages 141–145, May 2011. DOI: 10.1109/FCCM.2011.35 6

Ken Mai, Tim Paaske, Nuwan Jayasena, Ron Ho, William J. Dally, and Mark Horowitz. Smart memories: A modular reconfigurable architecture. In *Proc. 27th Symp. on Computer Architecture*, pages 161–171, June 2000. DOI: 10.1145/342001.339673 91

Robert McNaughton and Hisao Yamada. Regular expressions and state graphs for automata. *IEEE Trans. Electr. Comp.*, 9:39–47, 1960. DOI: 10.1109/TEC.1960.5221603 52

Ahmed Metwally, Divyakant Agrawal, and Amr El Abbadi. An integrated efficient solution for computing frequent and top-k elements in data streams. *ACM Trans. Database Syst.*, 31(3): 1095–1133, September 2006. DOI: 10.1145/1166074.1166084 46, 47

Abhishek Mitra, Marcos R. Vieira, Petko Bakalov, Vassilis J. Tsotras, and Walid A. Najjar. Boosting XML filtering through a scalable FPGA-based architecture. In *Proc. 4th Biennial Conf. on Innovative Data Systems Research*, January 2009. 69

Roger Moussalli, Mariam Salloum, Walid A. Najjar, and Vassilis J. Tsotras. Massively parallel XML twig filtering using dynamic programming on FPGAs. In *Proc. 27th Int. Conf. on Data Engineering*, pages 948–959, April 2011. DOI: 10.1109/ICDE.2011.5767899 69

Rene Mueller, Jens Teubner, and Gustavo Alonso. Streams on wires—a query compiler for FPGAs. *Proc. VLDB Endowment*, 2(1):229–240, August 2009. 62, 63, 65, 66

Rene Mueller, Jens Teubner, and Gustavo Alonso. Glacier: A query-to-hardware compiler. In *Proc. ACM SIGMOD Int. Conf. on Management of Data*, pages 1159–1162, June 2010. DOI: 10.1145/1807167.1807307 62

Rene Mueller, Jens Teubner, and Gustavo Alonso. Sorting networks on FPGAs. *VLDB J.*, 21 (1):1–23, February 2012. DOI: 10.1007/s00778-011-0232-z 71, 72, 73

Rasmus Pagh and Flemming Friche Rodler. Cuckoo hashing. In *Proc. 9th European Symp. on Algorithms*, pages 121–133, August 2001. DOI: 10.1007/978-0-387-30162-4_97 66

Sungwoo Park, Taekyung Kim, Jonghyun Park, Jinha Kim, and Hyeonseung Im. Parallel skyline computation on multicore architectures. In *Proc. 25th Int. Conf. on Data Engineering*, 2009. DOI: 10.1109/ICDE.2009.42 80, 81

Oliver Pell and Vitali Averbukh. Maximum performance computing with dataflow engines. *Computing in Science and Engineering*, 14(4):98–103, 2012. DOI: 10.1109/MCSE.2012.78 49

Mohammad Sadoghi, Harsh Singh, and Hans-Arno Jacobsen. Towards highly parallel event processing through reconfigurable hardware. In *Proc. 7th Workshop on Data Management on New Hardware*, pages 27–32, June 2011. DOI: 10.1145/1995441.1995445 69

David Schneider. The microsecond market. *IEEE Spectrum*, 49(6):66–81, June 2012. DOI: 10.1109/MSPEC.2012.6203974 62

Reetinder Sidhu and Viktor K. Prasanna. Fast regular expression matching using FPGAs. In *Proc. 9th IEEE Symp. on Field-Programmable Custom Computing Machines*, pages 227–238, April 2001. DOI: 10.1109/FCCM.2001.22 54

Satnam Singh. Computing without processors. *Commun. ACM*, 54(8):46–54, August 2011. DOI: 10.1145/1978542.1978558 41

Michael Stonebraker, Samuel Madden, Daniel J. Abadi, Stavros Harizopoulos, Nabil Hachem, and Pat Helland. The end of an architectural era: (it's time for a complete rewrite). In *Proc. 33rd Int. Conf. on Very Large Data Bases*, pages 1150–1160, 2007. 4

Tabula, Inc. Spacetime™ architecture, 2010. URL http://www.tabula.com/. White Paper. 68

Michael B. Taylor. Is dark silicon useful? harnessing the four horsemen of the coming dark silicon apocalypse. In *Proc. 49th Design Automaton Conference*, June 2012. DOI: 10.1145/2228360.2228567 89

Jens Teubner and Louis Woods. Snowfall: Hardware stream analysis made easy. In *Proc. 14th Conf. on Databases in Business, Technology, and Web*, pages 738–741, March 2011. 67

Jens Teubner, Rene Mueller, and Gustavo Alonso. Frequent item computation on a chip. *IEEE Trans. Knowl. and Data Eng.*, 23(8):1169–1181, August 2011. DOI: 10.1109/TKDE.2010.216 46, 47, 48

Jens Teubner, Louis Woods, and Chongling Nie. Skeleton automata for FPGAs: Reconfiguring without reconstructing. In *Proc. ACM SIGMOD Int. Conf. on Management of Data*, pages 229–240, May 2012. DOI: 10.1145/2213836.2213863 36, 45

Ken Thompson. Programming techniques: Regular expression search algorithm. *Commun. ACM*, 11(6):419–422, 1968. DOI: 10.1145/363347.363387 52

Maamar Touiza, Gilberto Ochoa-Ruiz, El-Bay Bourennane, Abderrezak Guessoum, and Kamel Messaoudi. A novel methodology for accelerating bitstream relocation in partially reconfigurable systems. *Microprocessors and Microsystems*, 2012. DOI: 10.1016/j.micpro.2012.07.004 30

Philipp Unterbrunner, Georgios Giannikis, Gustavo Alonso, Dietmar Fauser, and Donald Kossmann. Predictable performance for unpredictable workloads. *Proc. VLDB Endowment*, 2(1): 706–717, 2009. 62

Pranav Vaidya and Jaehwan John Lee. A novel multicontext coarse-grained reconfigurable architecture (CGRA) for accelerating column-oriented databases. *ACM Trans. Reconfig. Technol. Syst.*, 4(2), May 2011. DOI: 10.1145/1968502.1968504 38

Pranav Vaidya, Jaehwan John Lee, Francis Bowen, Yingzi Du, Chandima H. Nadungodage, and Yuni Xia. Symbiote: A reconfigurable logic assisted data stream management system (RLADSMS). In *Proc. ACM SIGMOD Int. Conf. on Management of Data*, pages 1147–1150, June 2010. DOI: 10.1145/1807167.1807304 70

Louis Woods, Jens Teubner, and Gustavo Alonso. Complex event detection at wire speed with FPGAs. *Proc. VLDB Endowment*, 3(1):660–669, September 2010. 58, 59, 60

Louis Woods, Jens Teubner, and Gustavo Alonso. Real-time pattern matching with FP-GAs. In *Proc. 27th Int. Conf. on Data Engineering*, pages 1292–1295, April 2011. DOI: 10.1109/ICDE.2011.5767937 59, 60

Louis Woods, Jens Teubner, and Gustavo Alonso. Parallel computation of skyline queries. In *Proc. 21st IEEE Symp. on Field-Programmable Custom Computing Machines*, April 2013. 77, 78, 79, 80, 81

Yi-Hua E. Yang and Viktor K. Prasanna. High-performance and compact architecture for regular expression matching on FPGA. *IEEE Trans. Comput.*, 61(7):1013–1025, July 2012. DOI: 10.1109/TC.2011.129 45, 55, 56

Yi-Hua E. Yang, Weirong Jiang, and Viktor K. Prasanna. Compact architecture for high-throughput regular expression matching on FPGA. In *Proc. ACM/IEEE Symp. on Architecture for Networking and Communication Systems*, pages 30–39, November 2008. DOI: 10.1145/1477942.1477948 46, 55, 56, 57, 58

Authors' Biographies

JENS TEUBNER

Jens Teubner is leading the Databases and Information Systems Group at TU Dortmund in Germany. His main research interest is data processing on modern hardware platforms, including FPGAs, multi-core processors, and hardware-accelerated networks. Previously, Jens Teubner was a postdoctoral researcher at ETH Zurich (2008–2013) and IBM Research (2007–2008). He holds a Ph.D. in Computer Science from TU München (Munich, Germany) and an M.S. degree in Physics from the University of Konstanz in Germany.

LOUIS WOODS

Louis Woods is a Ph.D. student, who joined the Systems Group at ETH Zurich in 2009. His research interests include FPGAs in the context of databases, modern hardware, stream processing, parallel algorithms, and design patterns. Louis Woods received both his B.S. and M.S. degree in Computer Science from ETH Zurich in 2008 and 2009, respectively.

Index